SWEET CANDY WOMEN

Coloring Book For Adults

Bibliographical Note
Sweet Candy Women Coloring Book is a new work,
first published by Amazon, Inc, in 2023

International Standard Book Number
ISBN: 9798867555764

Manufactured in US

Immerse yourself in a world where confectionery meets elegance with "Sweet Candy Women" an enchanting adult coloring book that brings together the allure of beautiful women and the irresistible charm of candies. This unique coloring experience offers a delightful collection of grayscale pages, each featuring realistic portraits of stunning candy-adorned women, meticulously designed to captivate your imagination.

Dive into the intricate details of these lifelike illustrations, where every curve and shadow is carefully crafted to create a canvas that awaits your artistic touch. The grayscale format adds a sophisticated twist, allowing you to explore a broad spectrum of shades and tones to breathe life into these sweet sirens. From luscious licorice dresses to decadent chocolate accessories, each page tells a story of sugary sophistication.

As you embark on your coloring journey, lose yourself in the intricacies of swirls and twirls, turning each page into a masterpiece of your own creation. Whether you prefer vibrant bursts of color or the subtlety of grayscale shading, "Sweet Candy Women" provides a satisfying and soothing coloring experience that caters to artists of all levels.

Indulge in the therapeutic benefits of adult coloring as you bring these candy women to life. Unleash your creativity, experiment with different color palettes, and watch as the captivating fusion of realism and confectionery whimsy unfolds before your eyes. "Sweet Candy Women" is more than just a coloring book; it's a celebration of the sweetest fantasies and the artistry within you.

Treat yourself to a delightful escape as you transform each page into a delectable masterpiece. Whether you're a coloring enthusiast or a newcomer seeking a unique artistic experience, "Sweet Candy Women" invites you to savor the joy of coloring and lose yourself in a world where beauty and sweetness intertwine in perfect harmony.

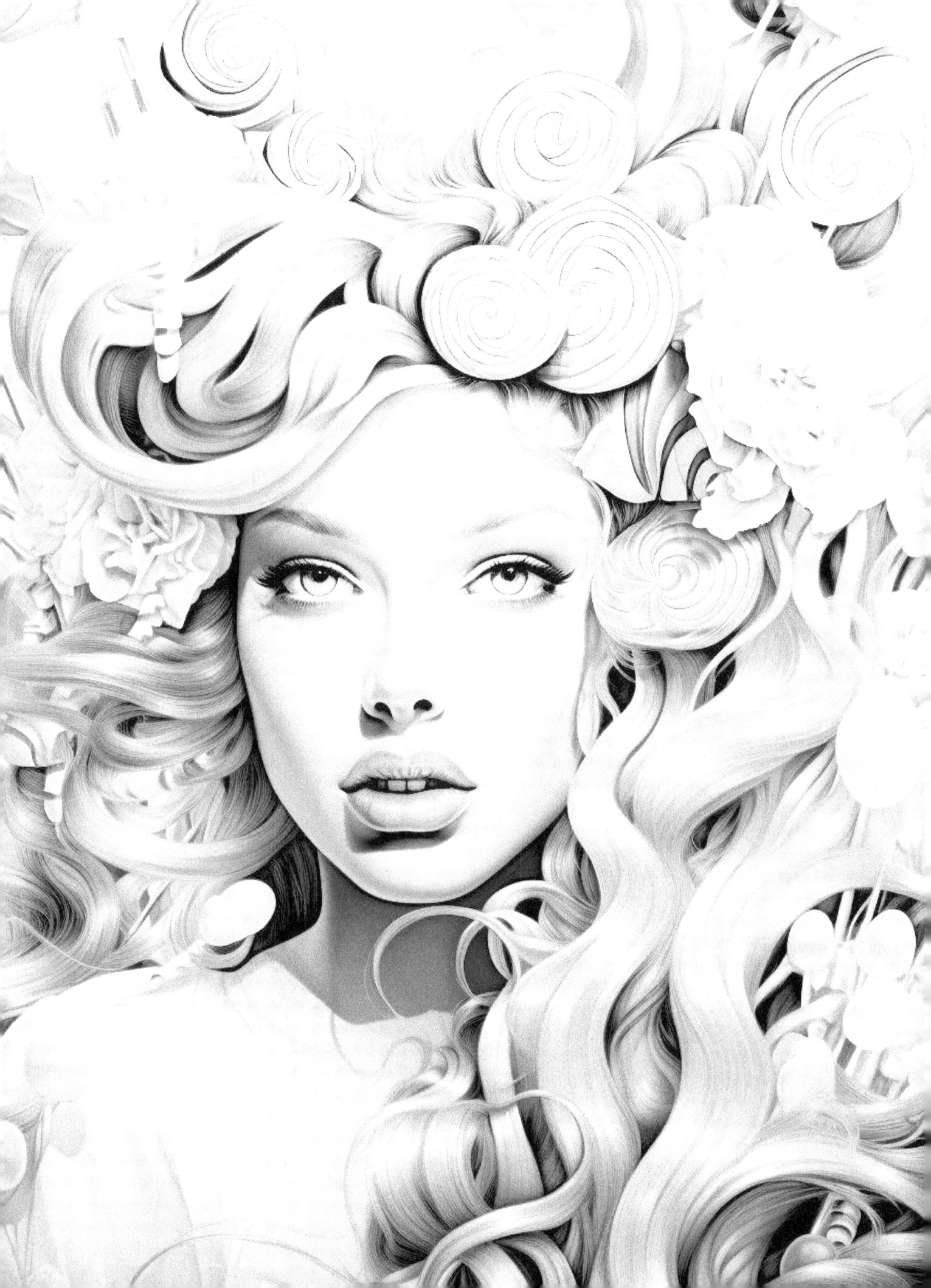

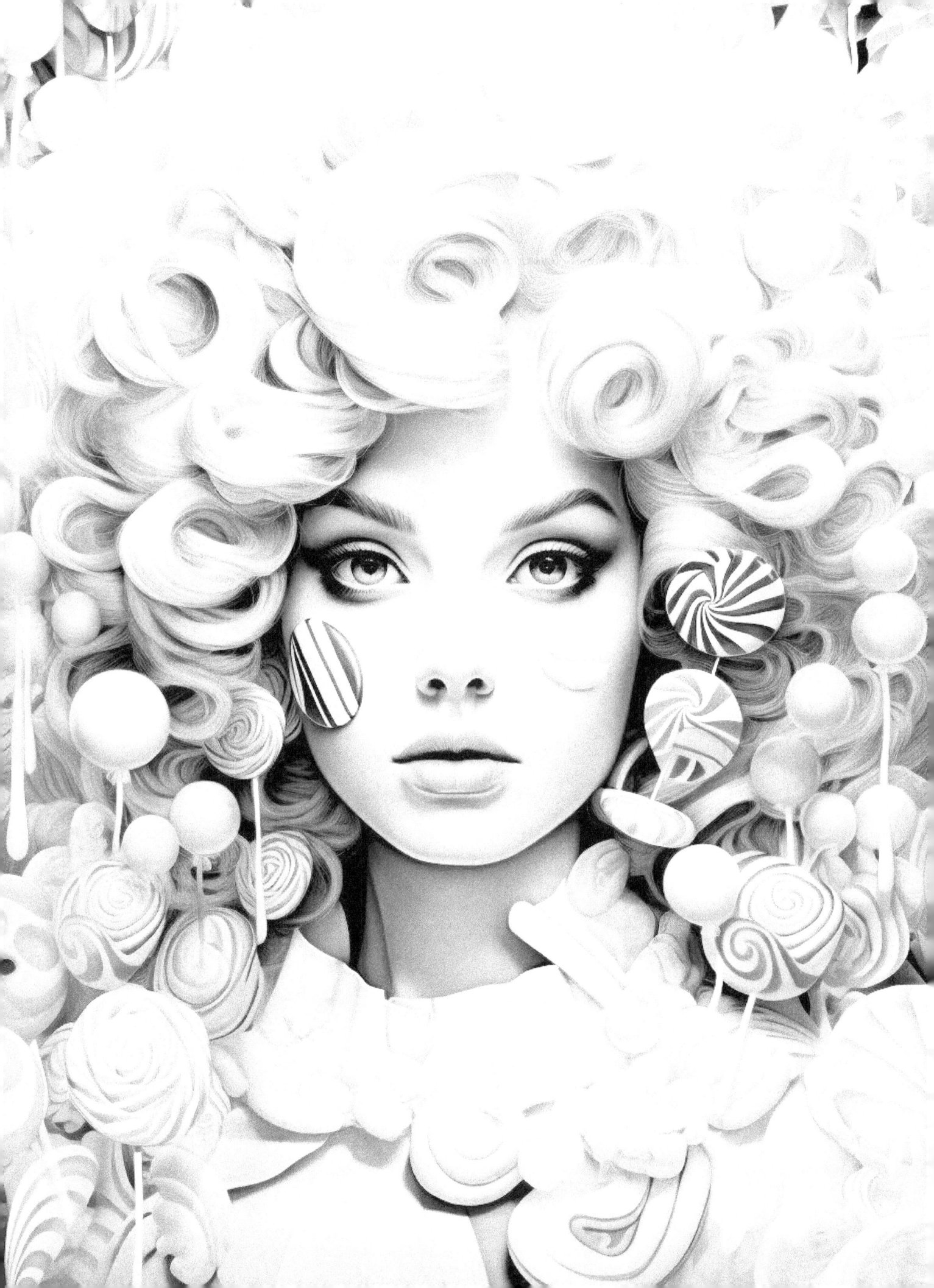

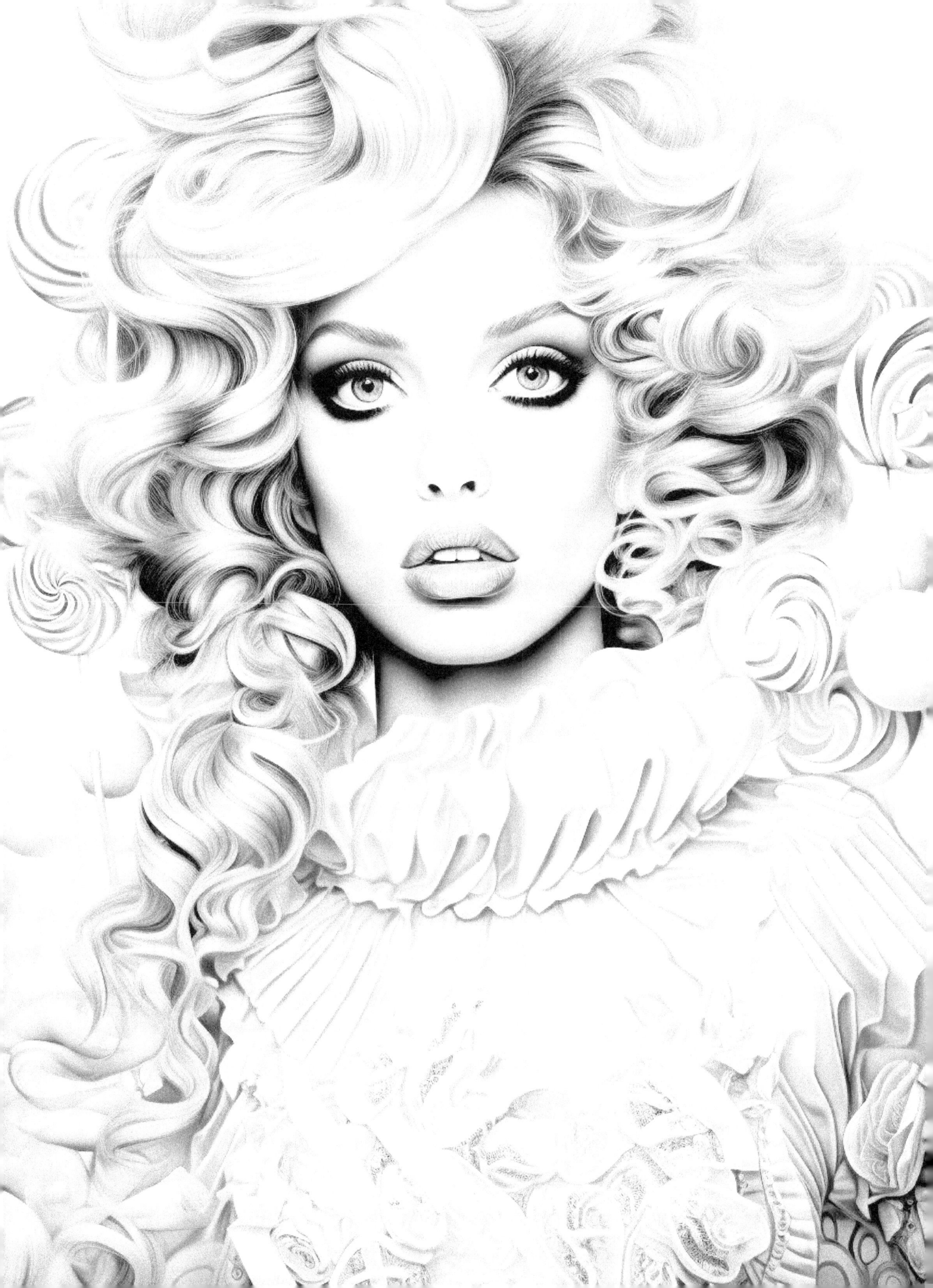

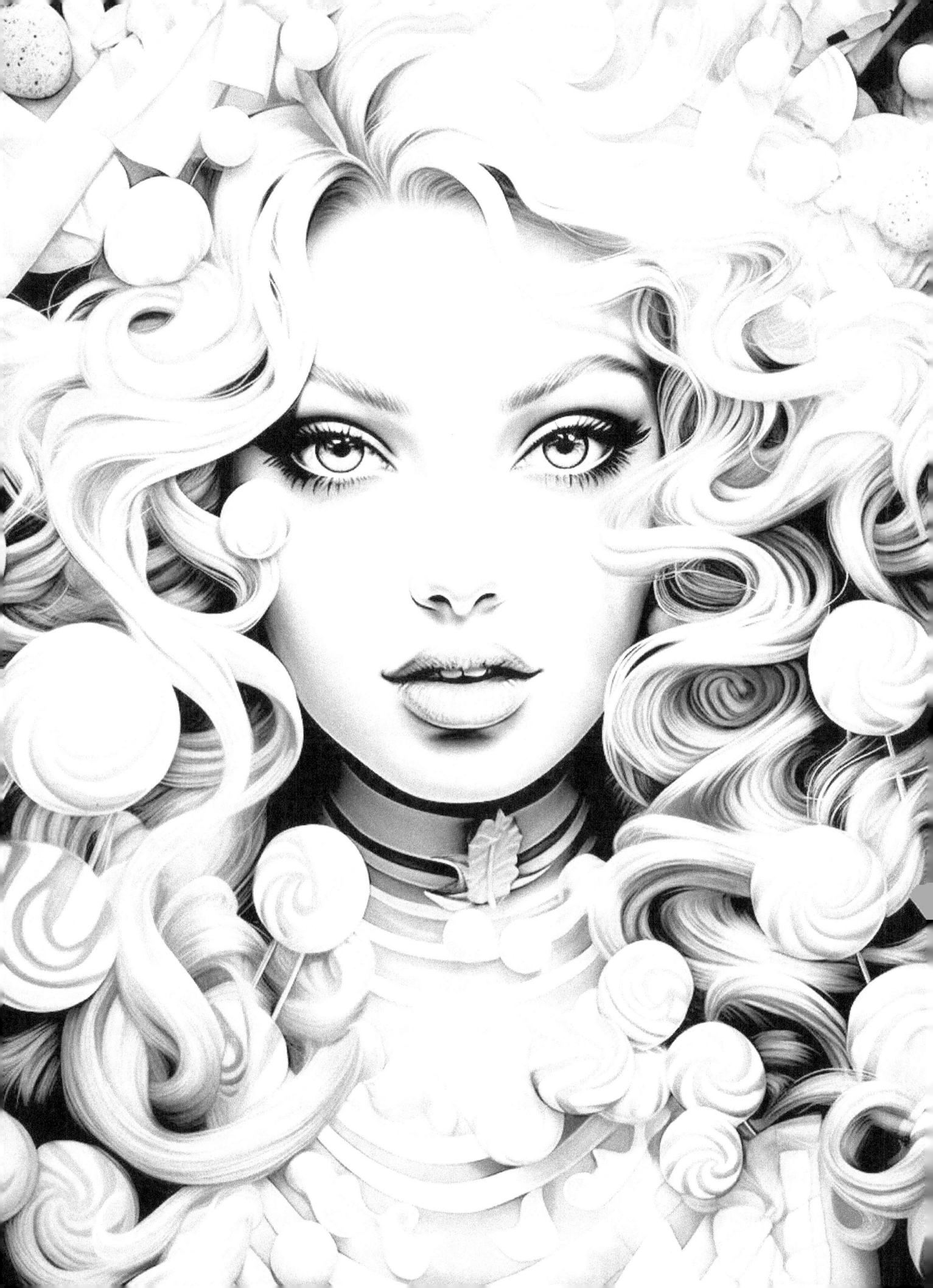

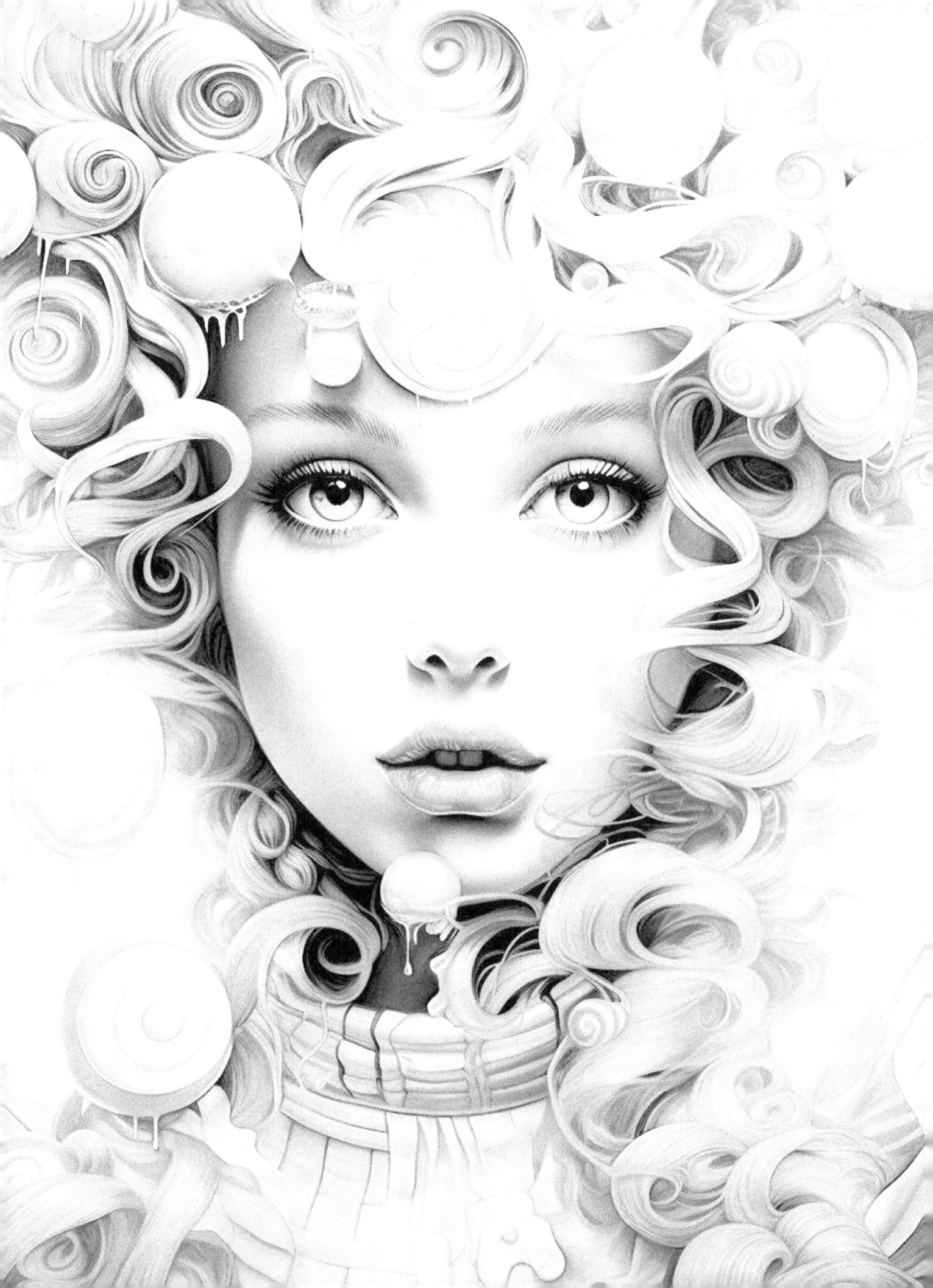

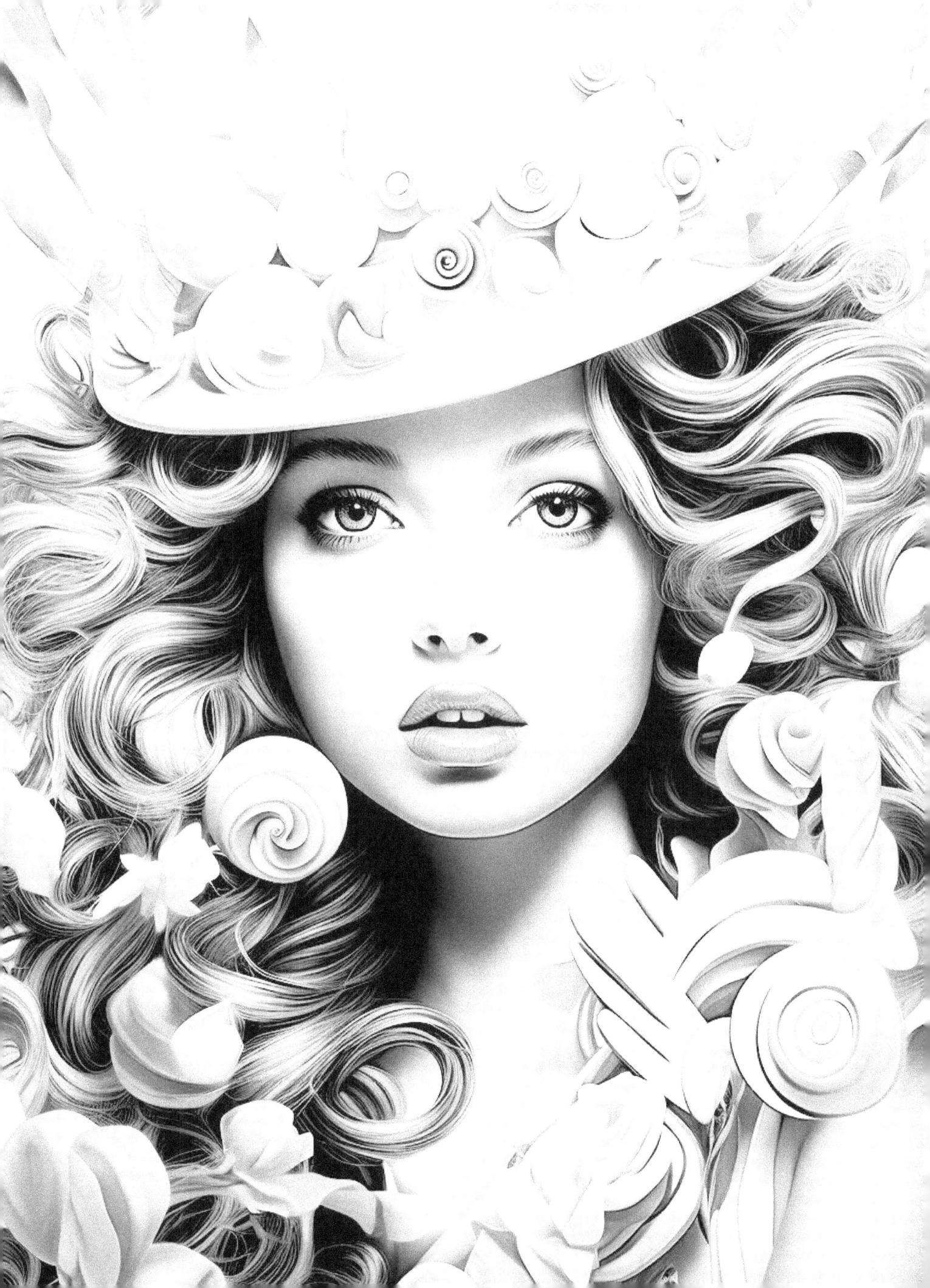

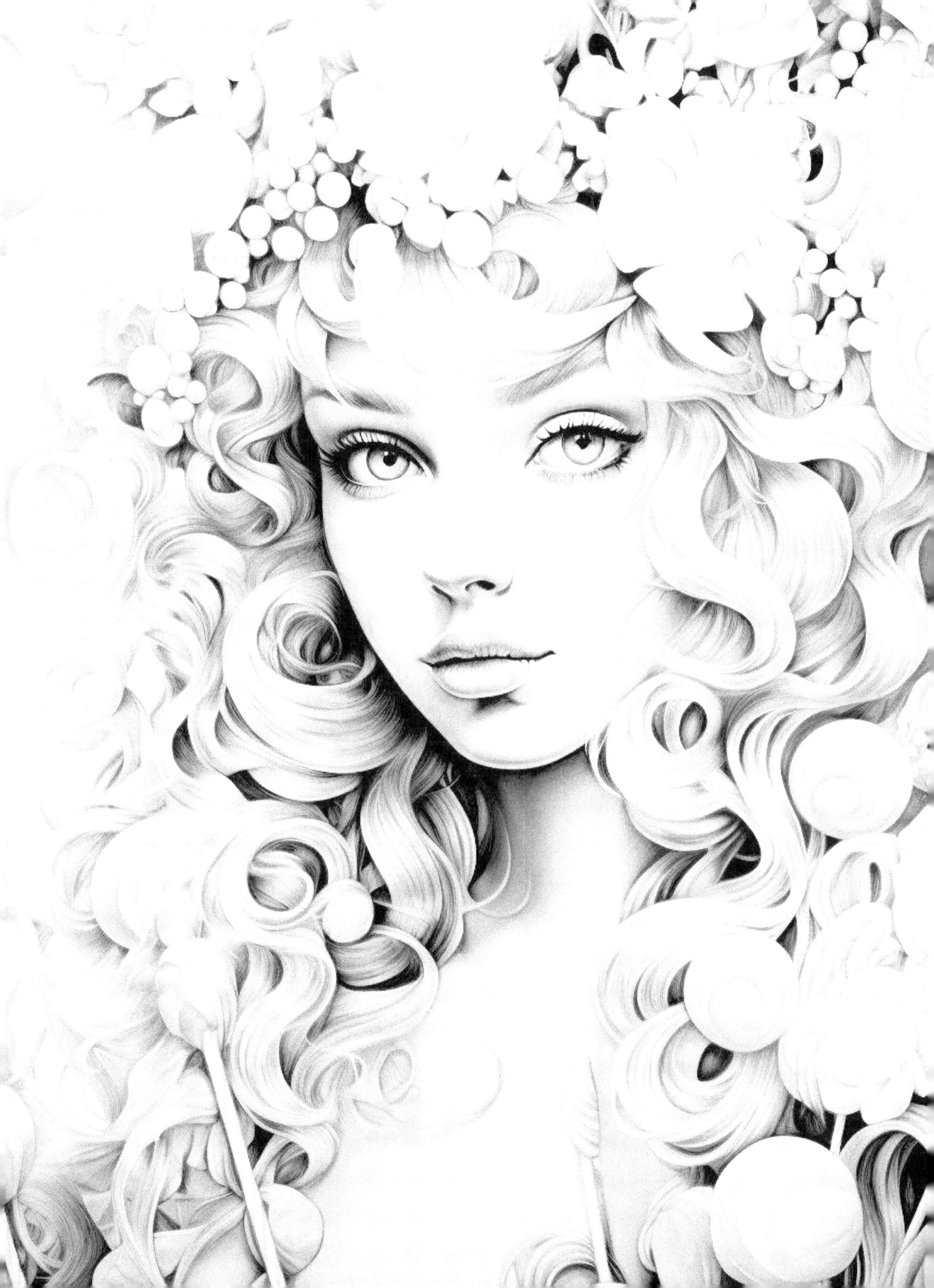

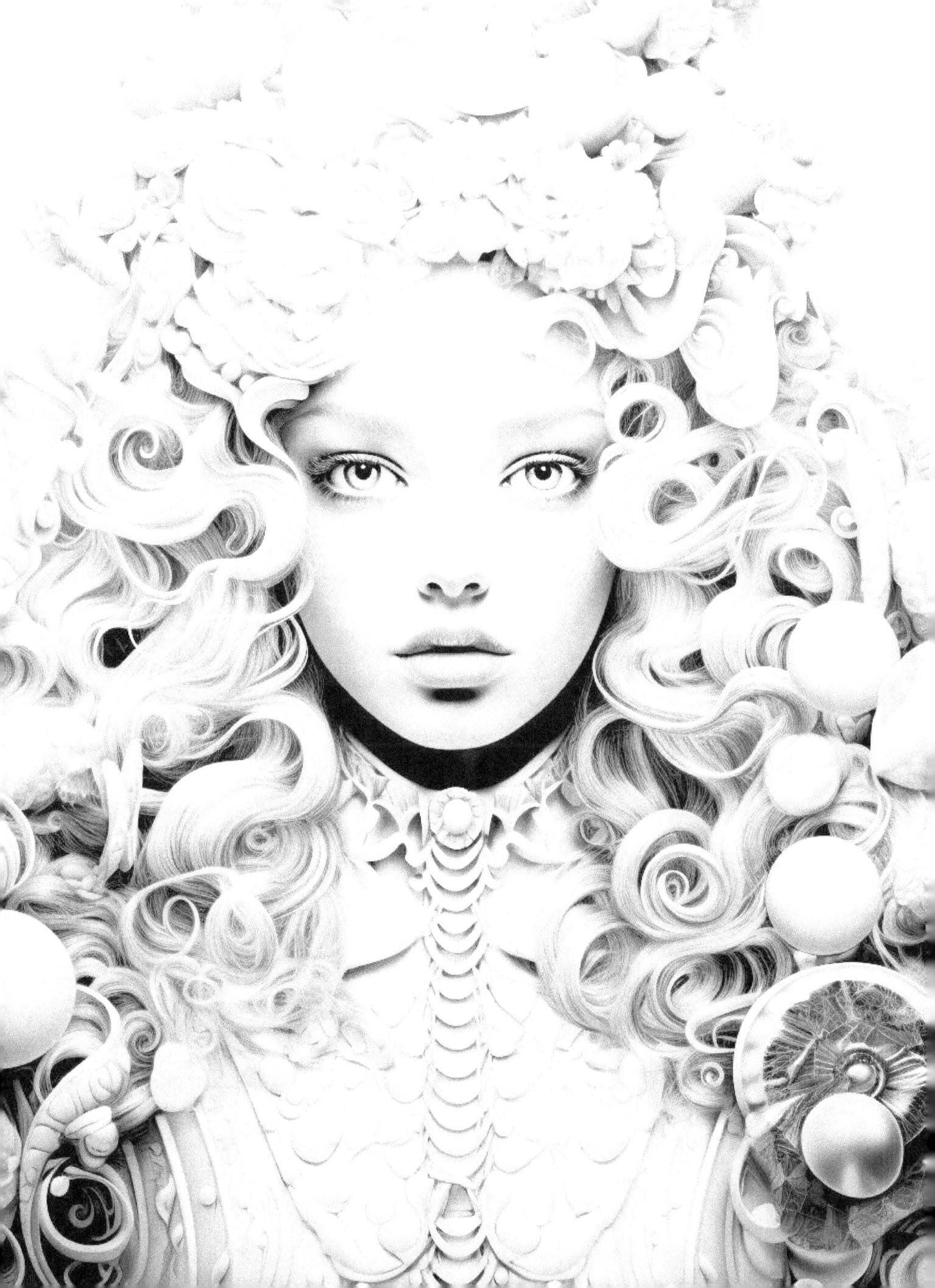

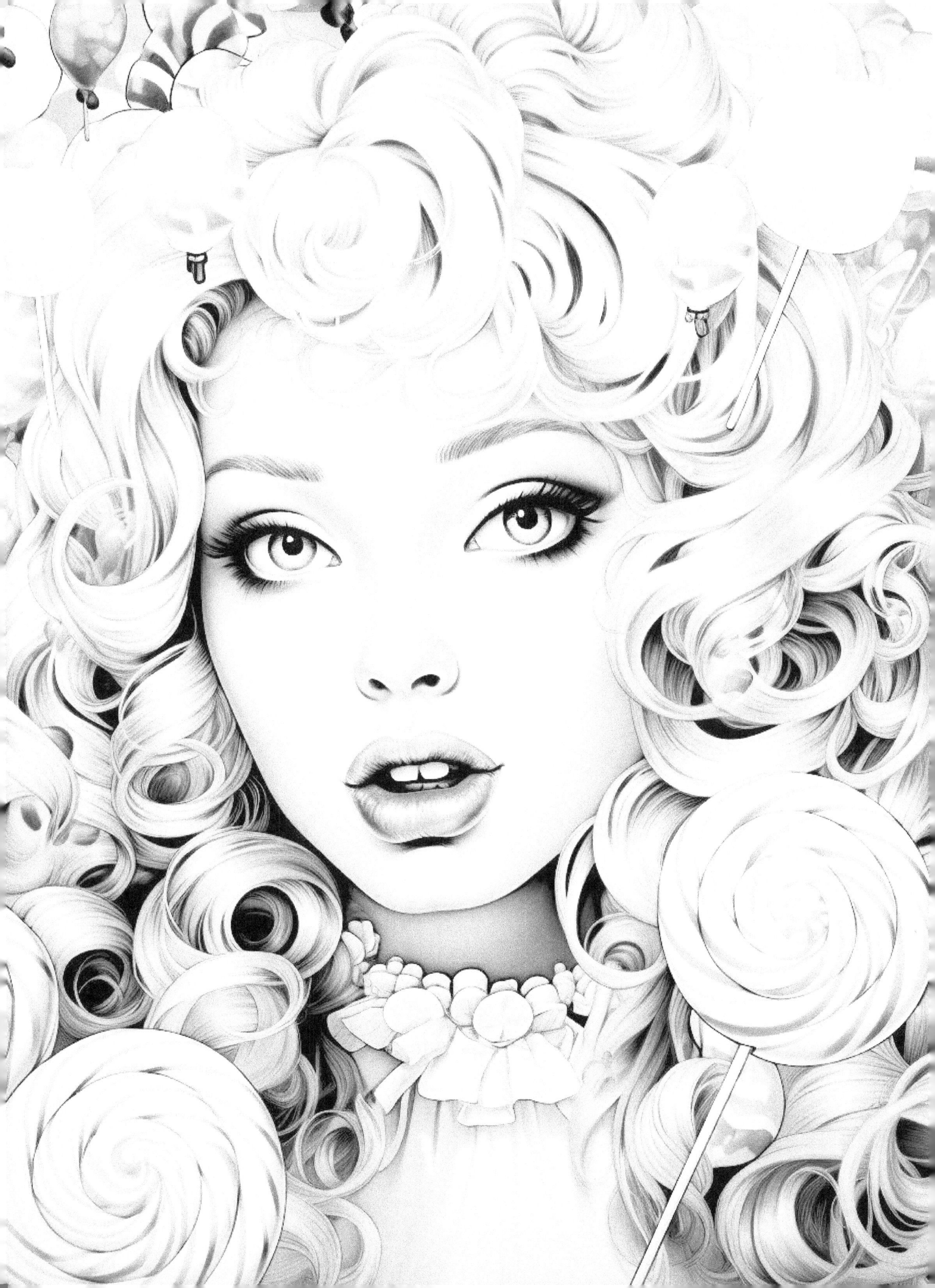

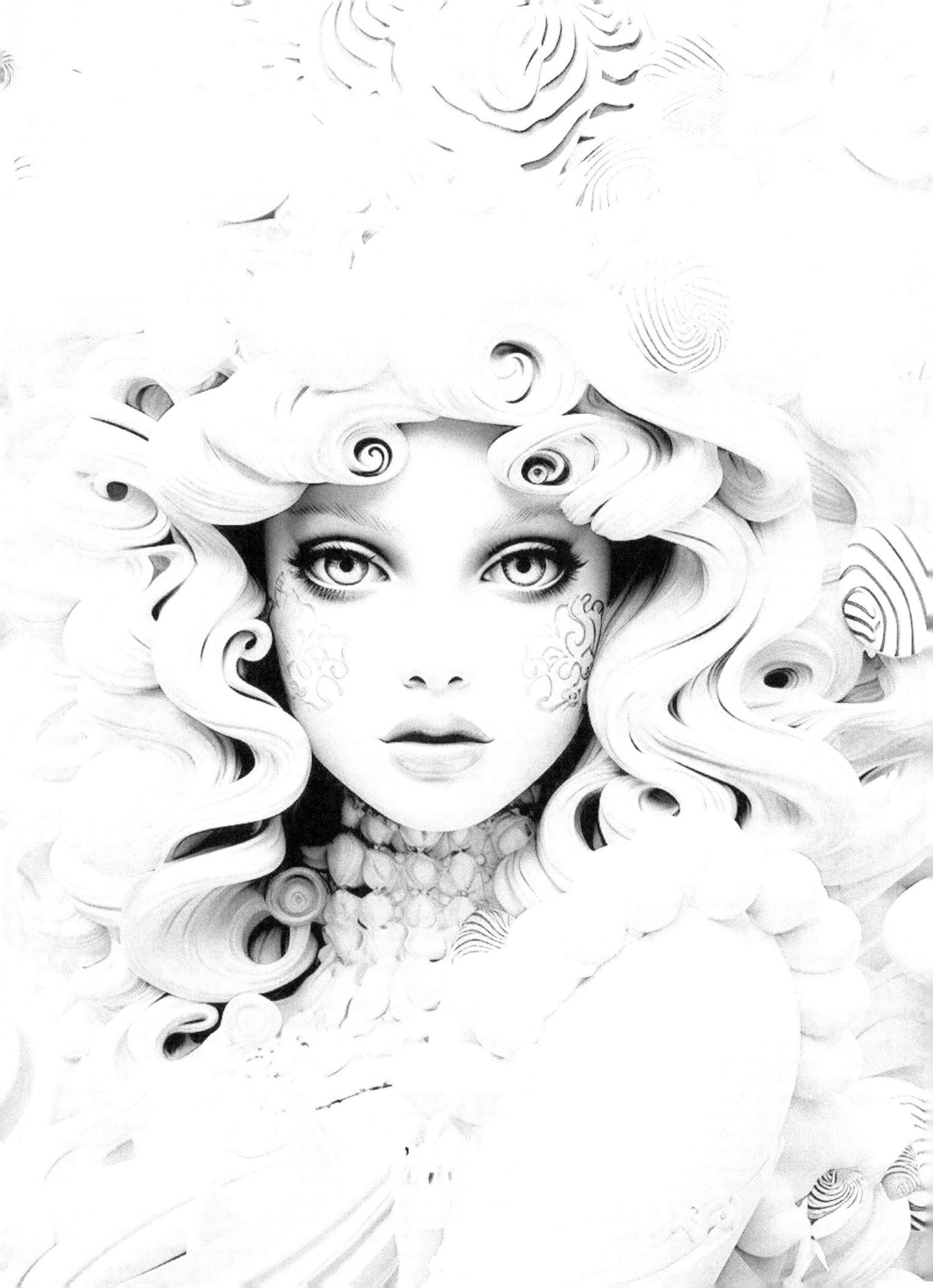

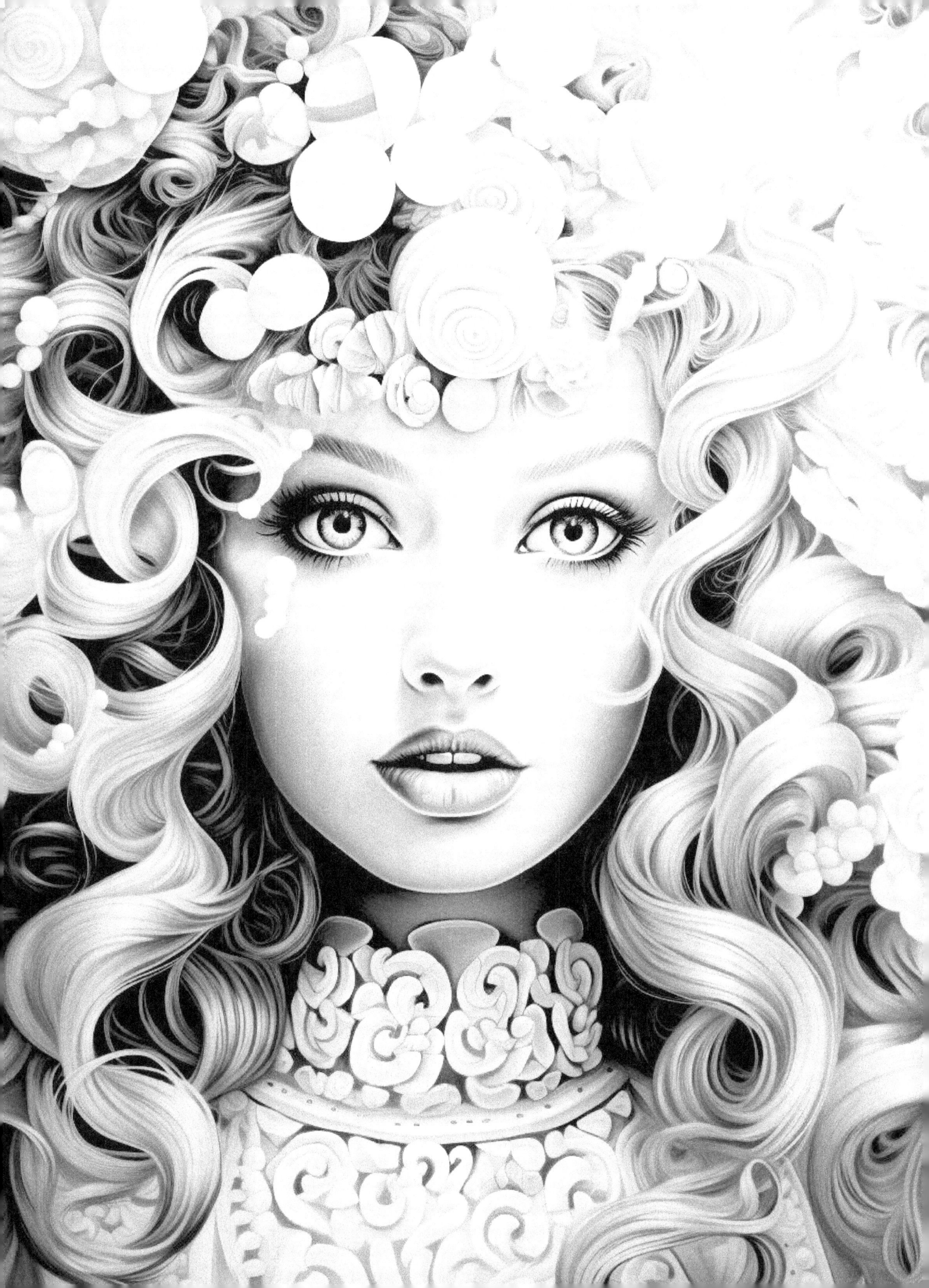

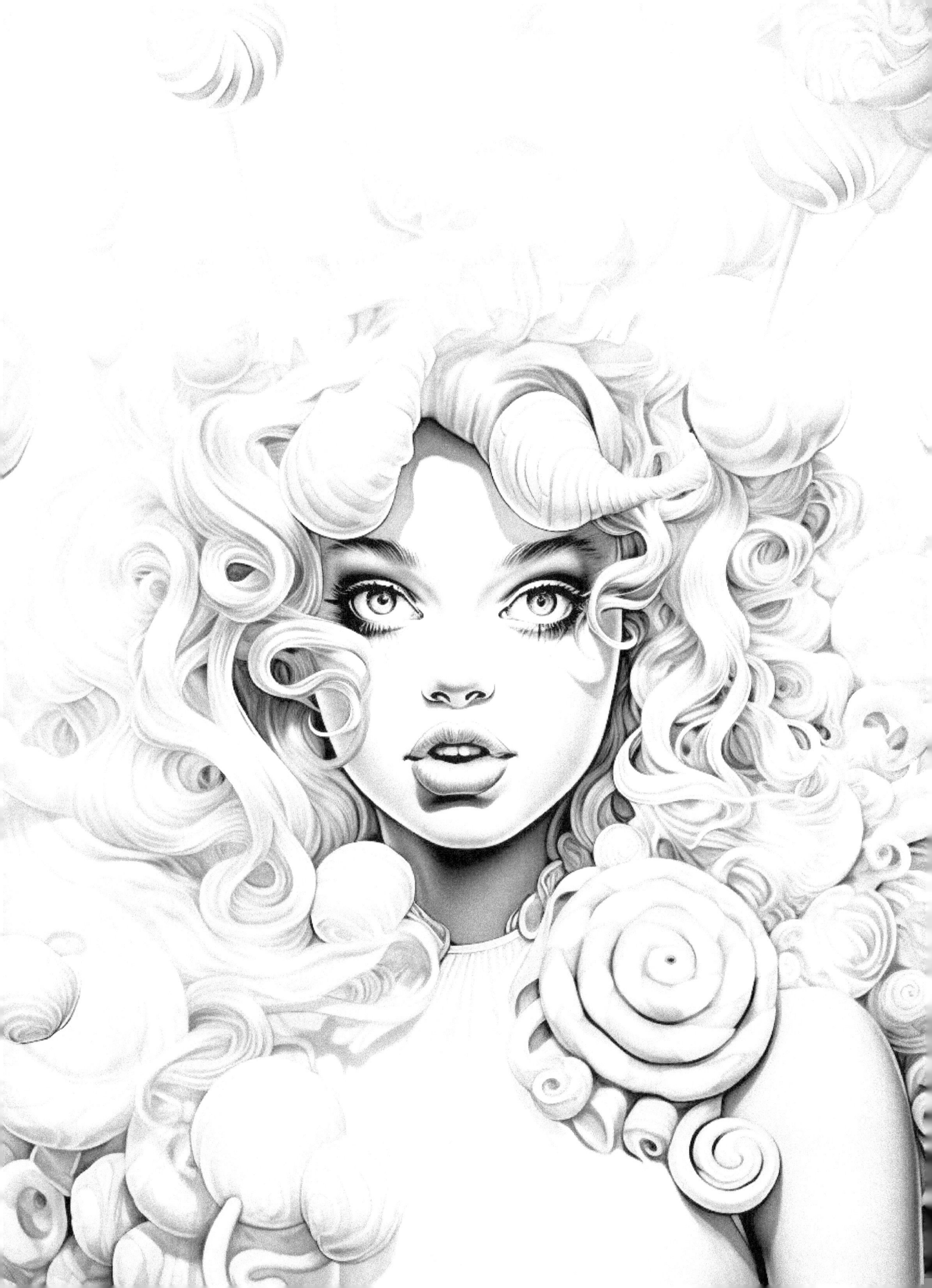

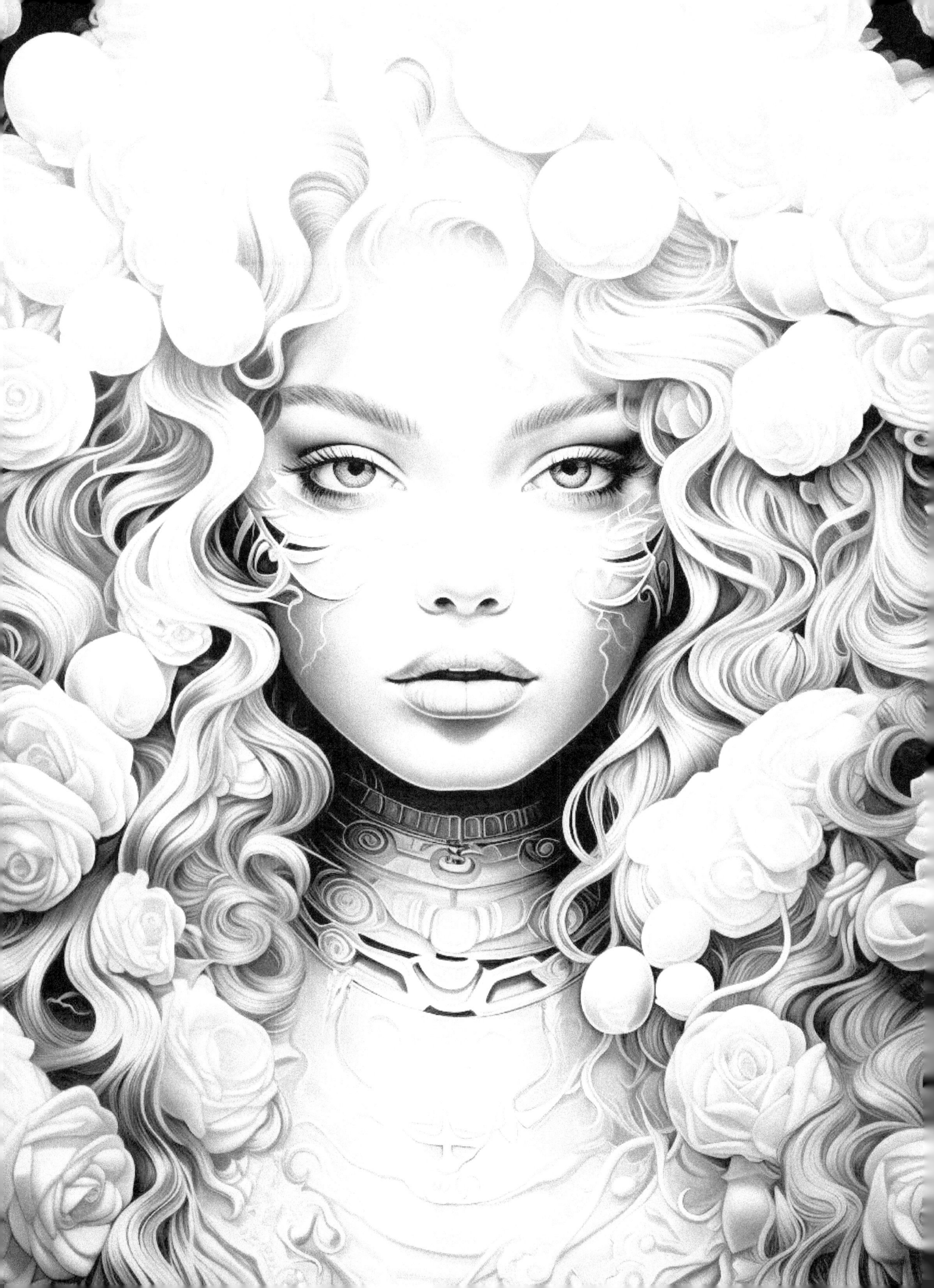

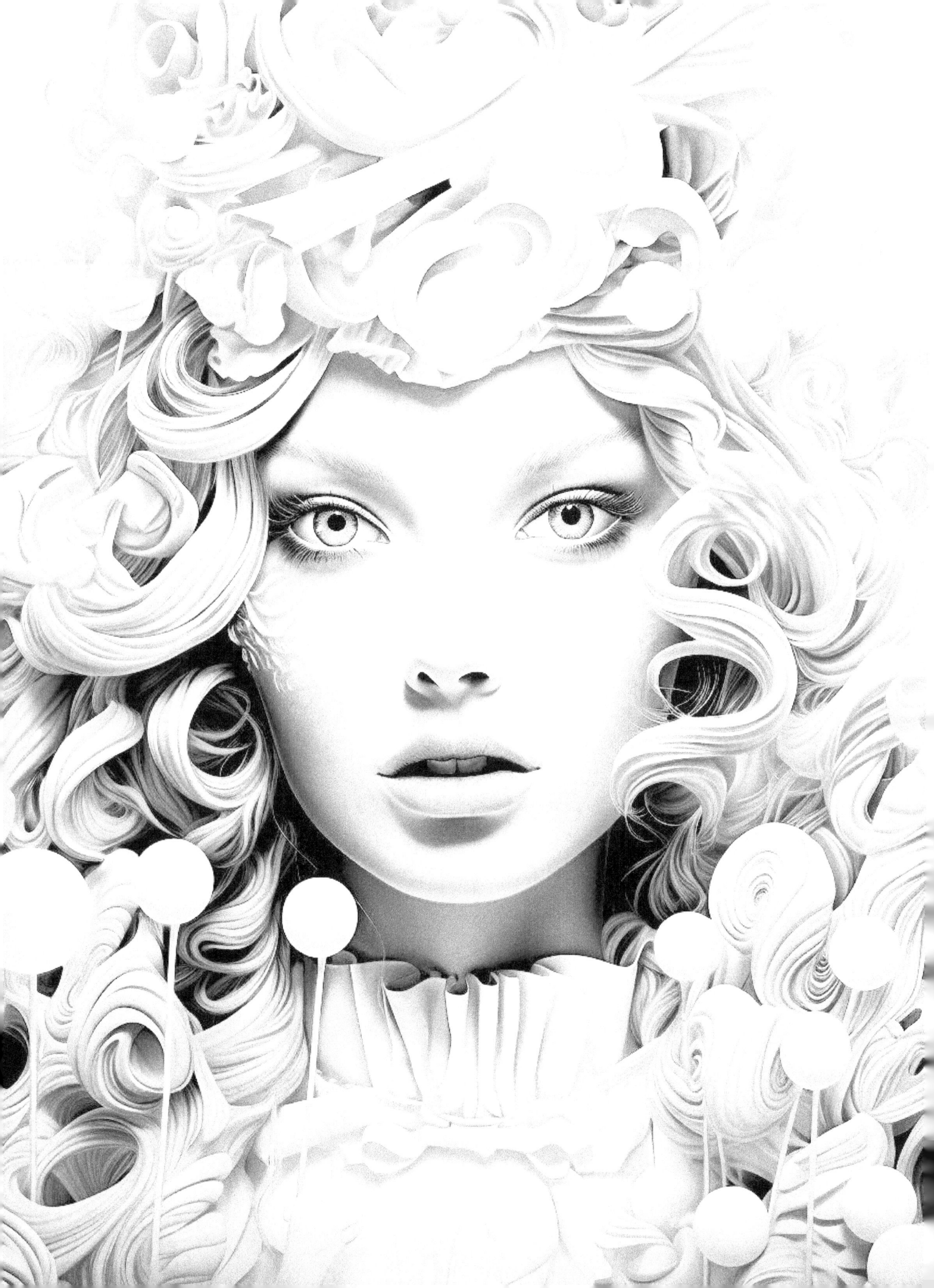

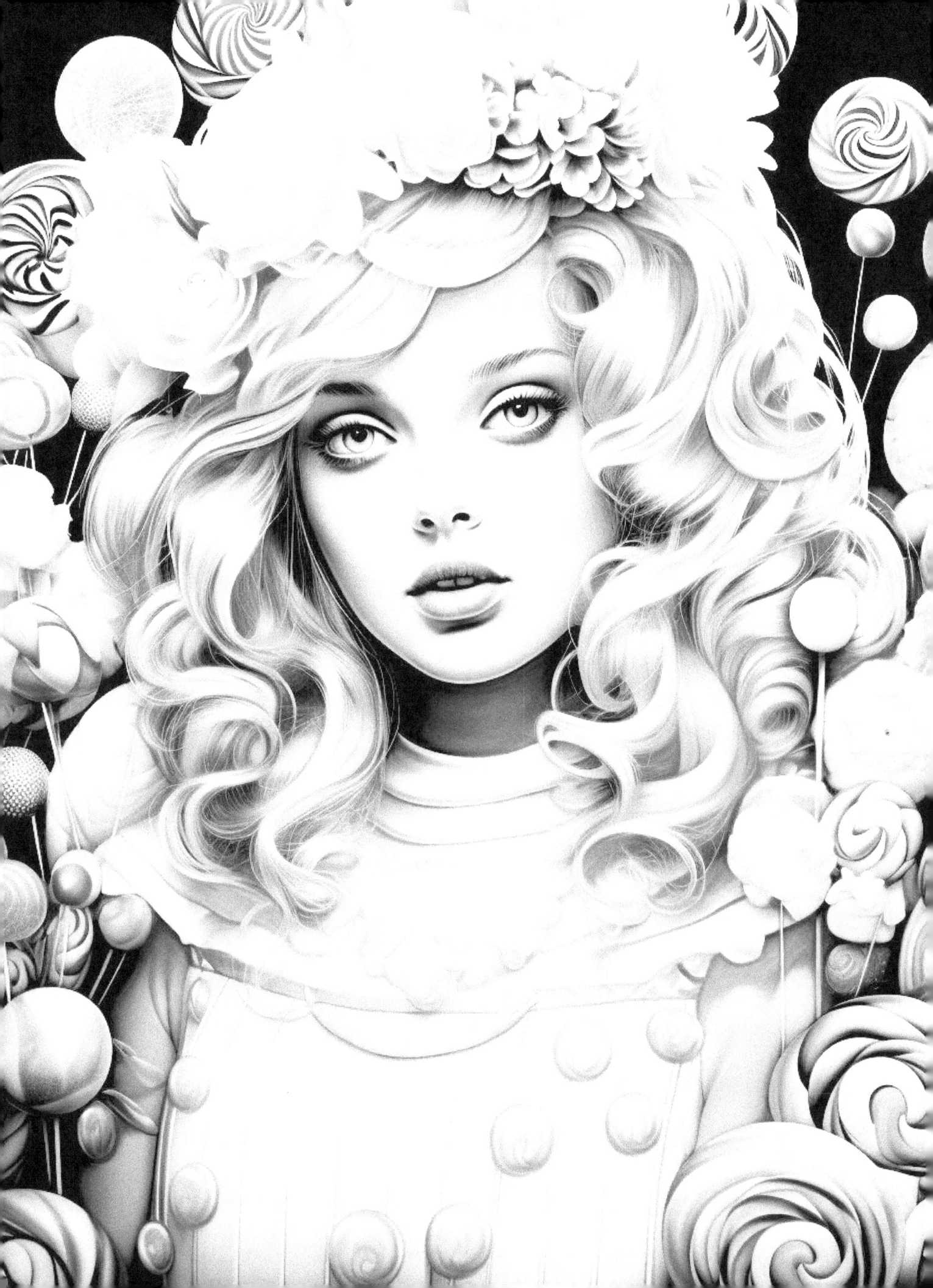

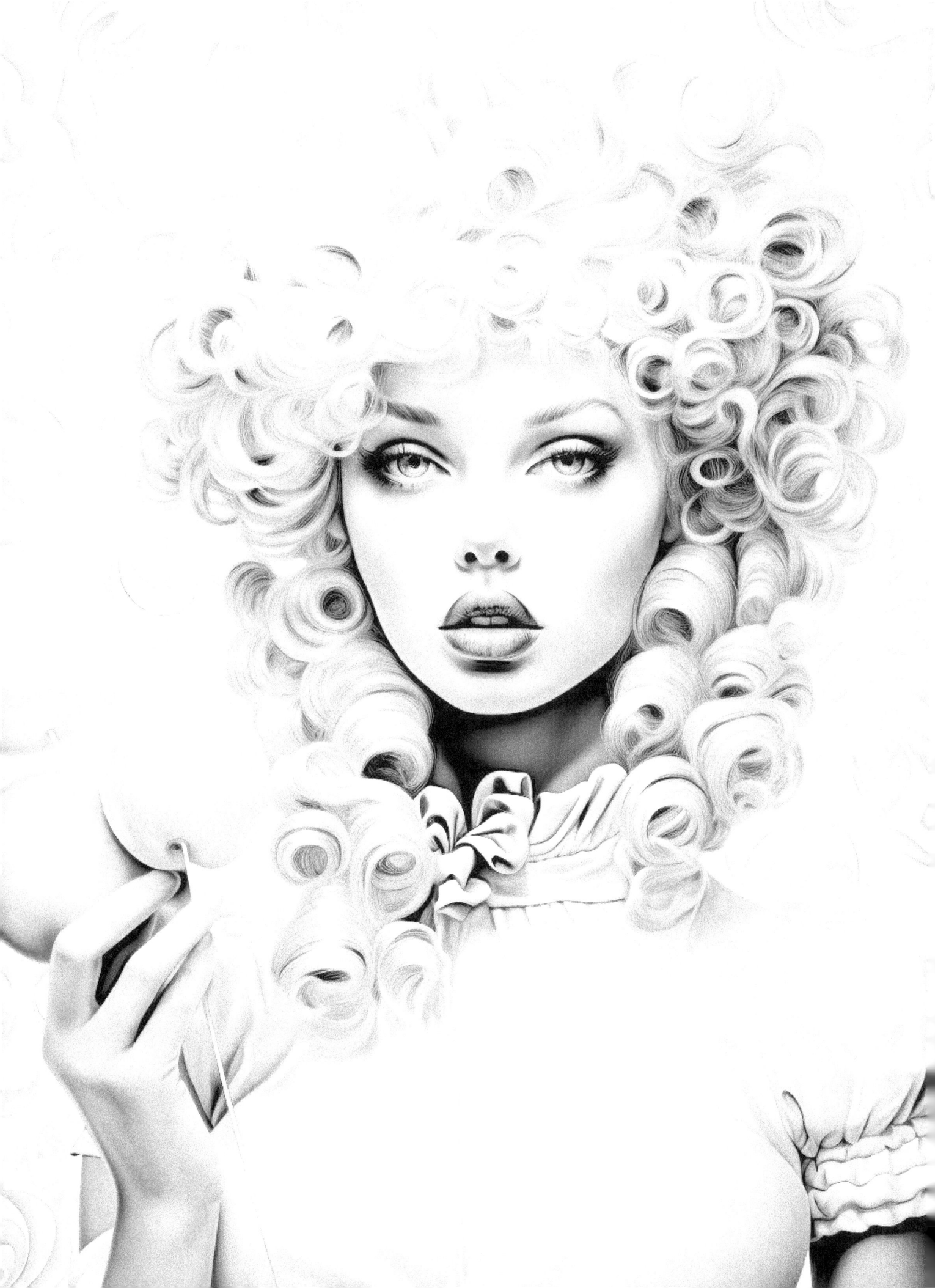

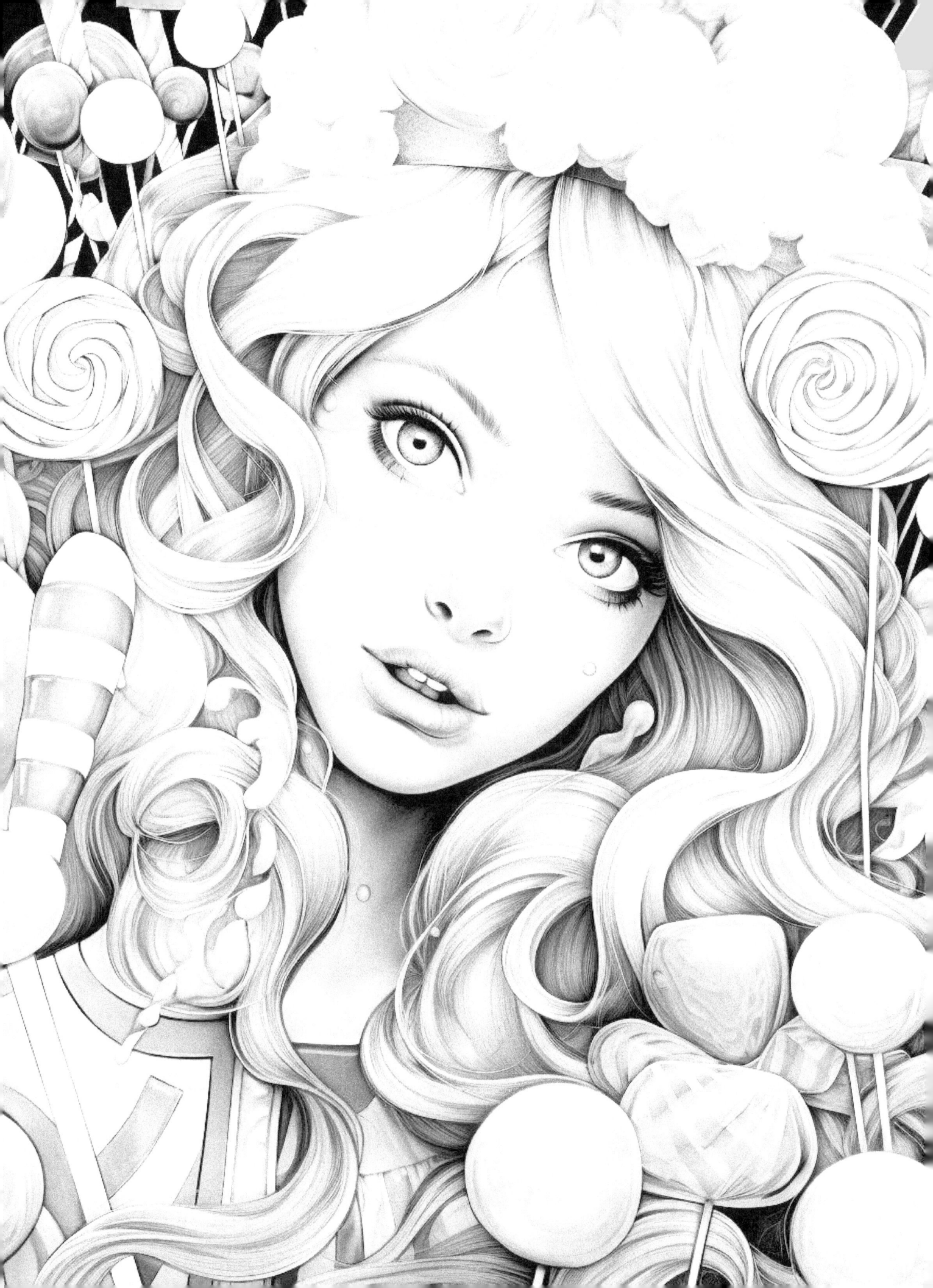

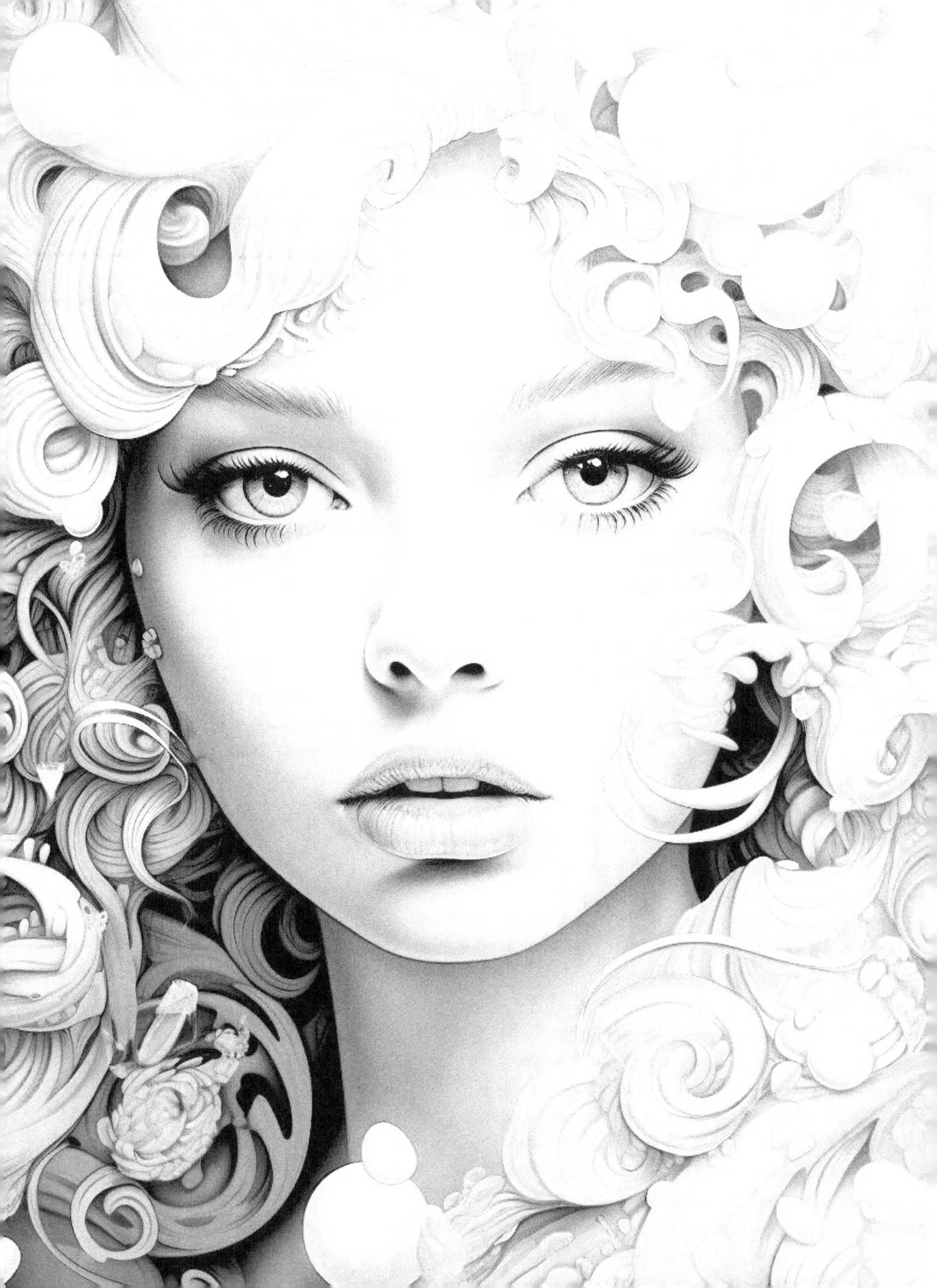

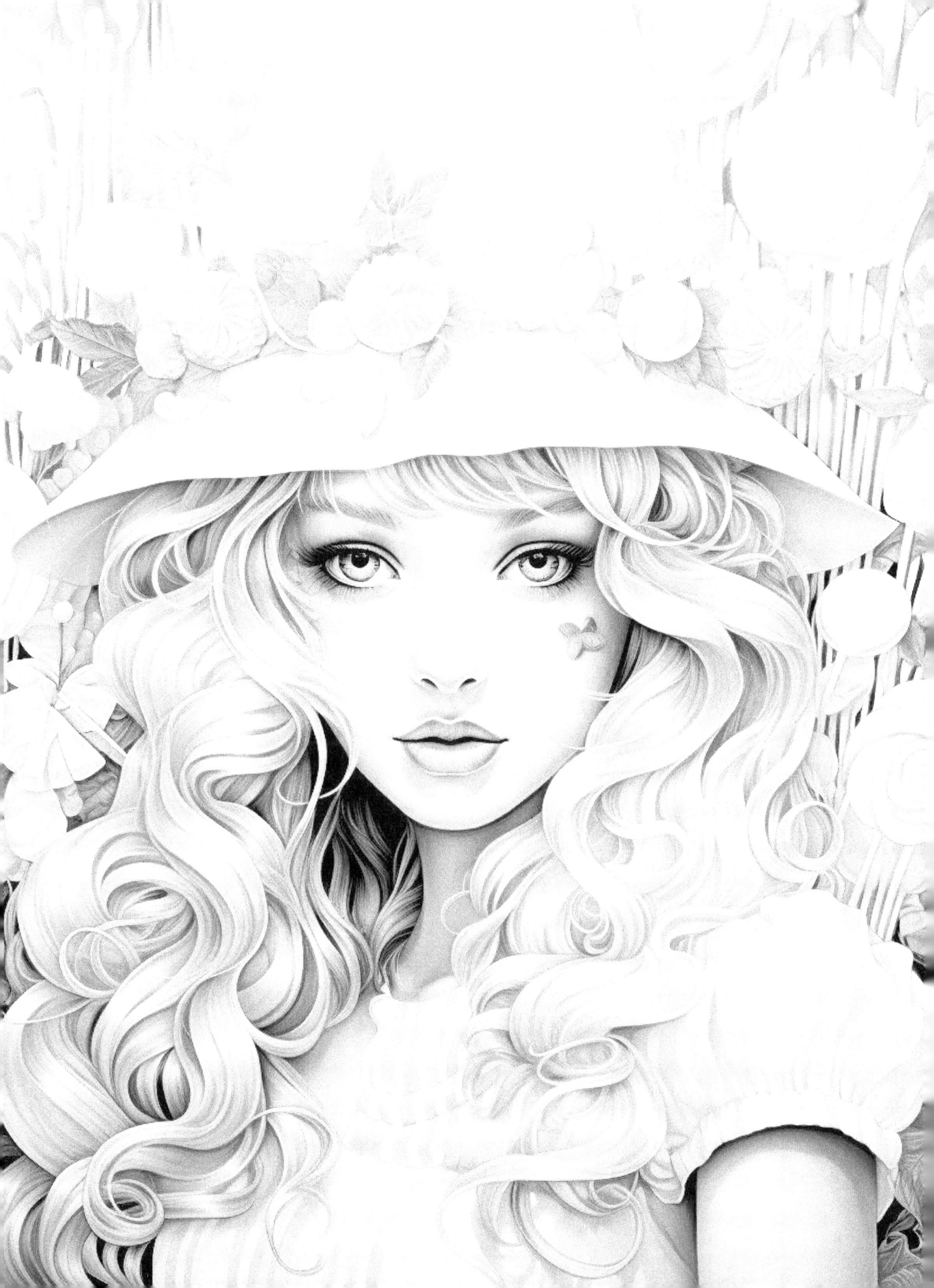

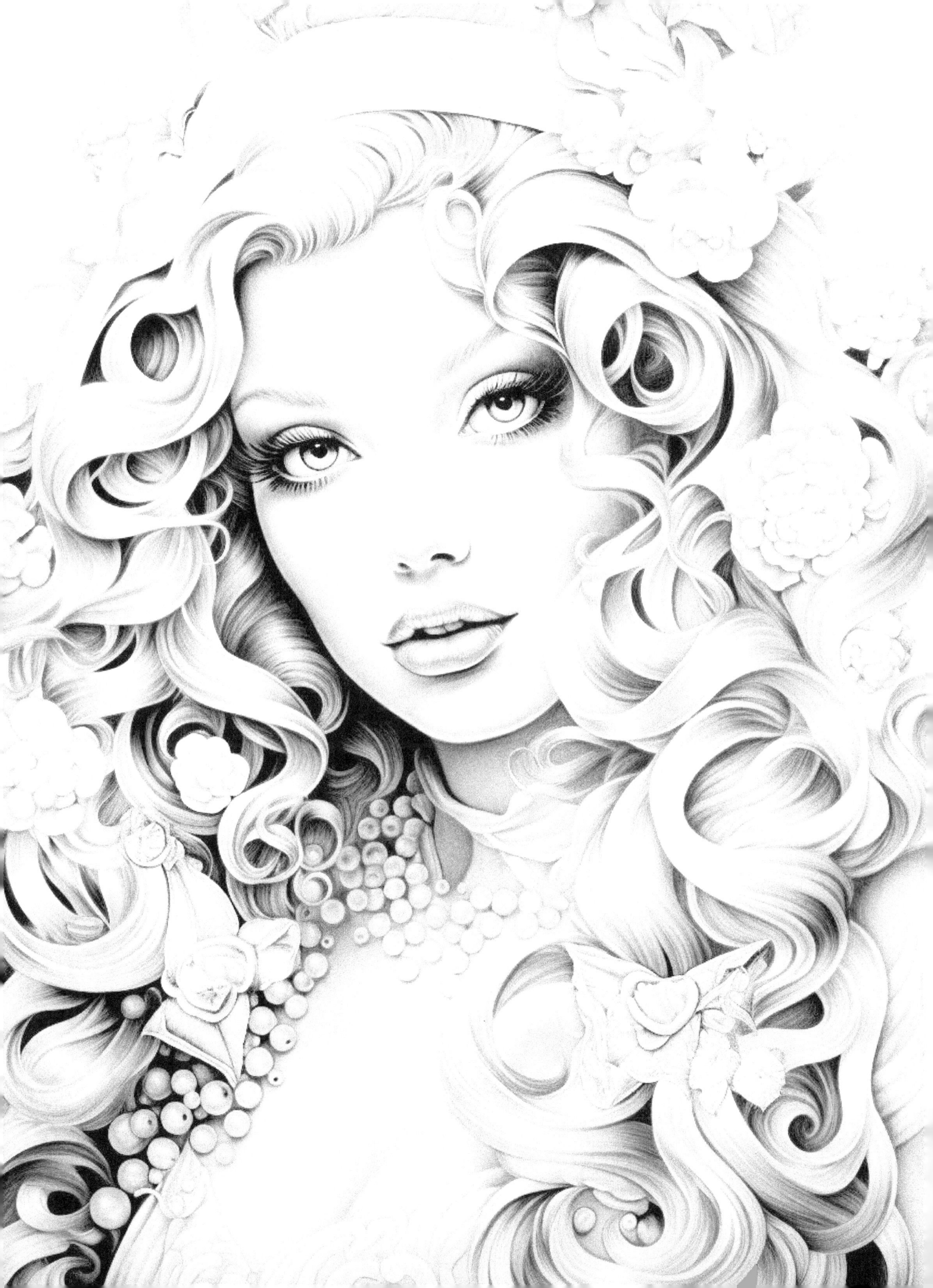

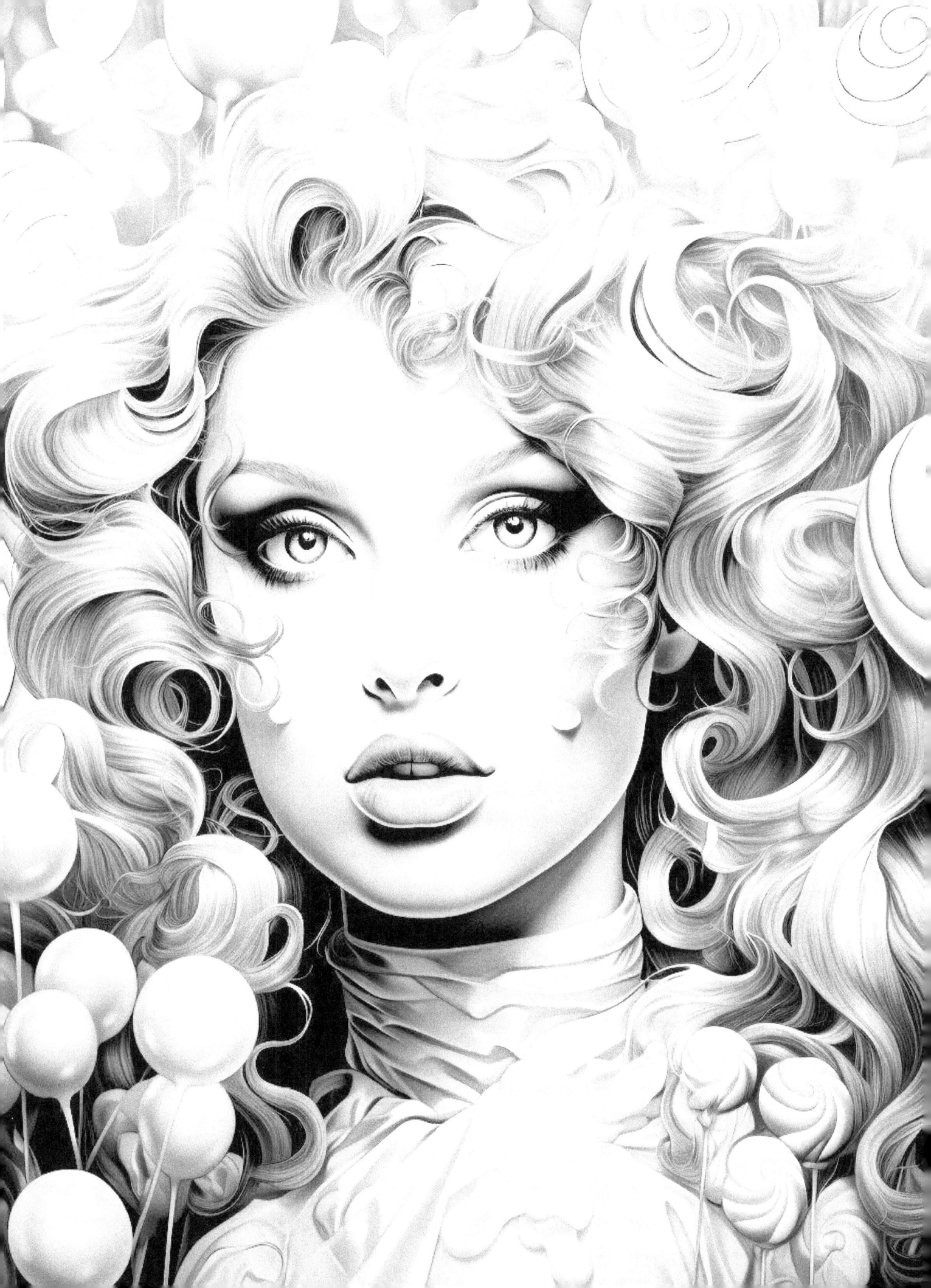

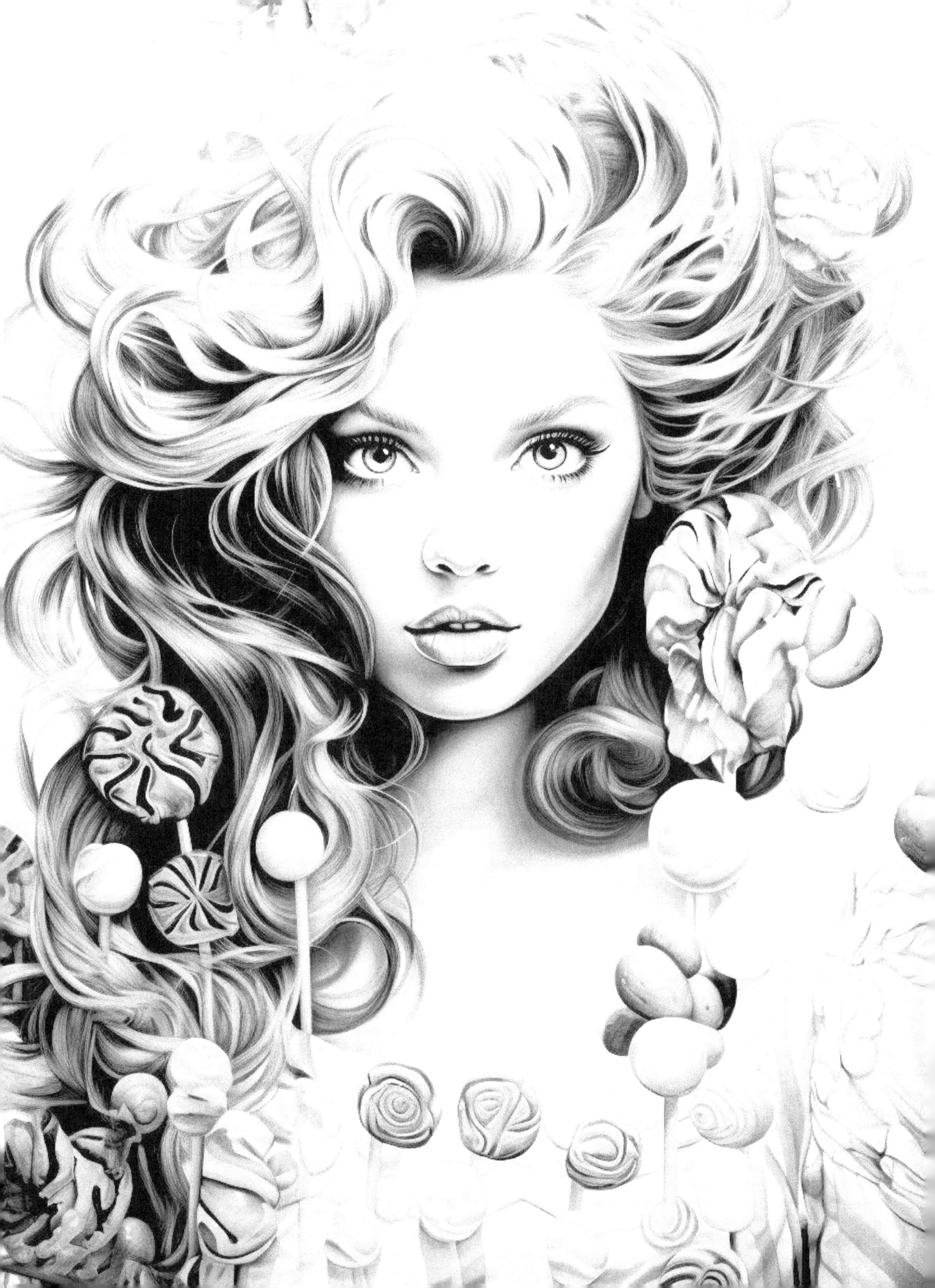

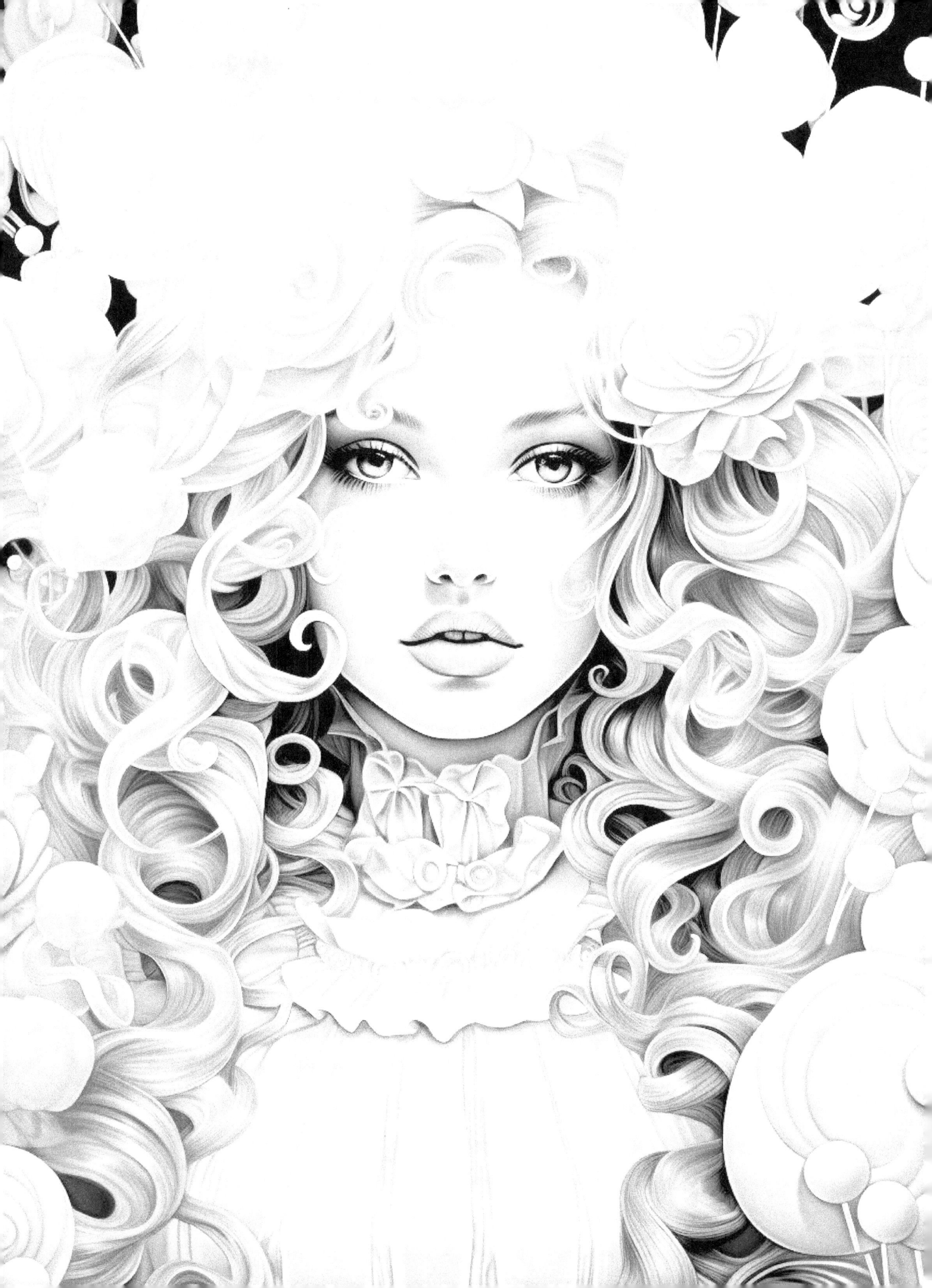

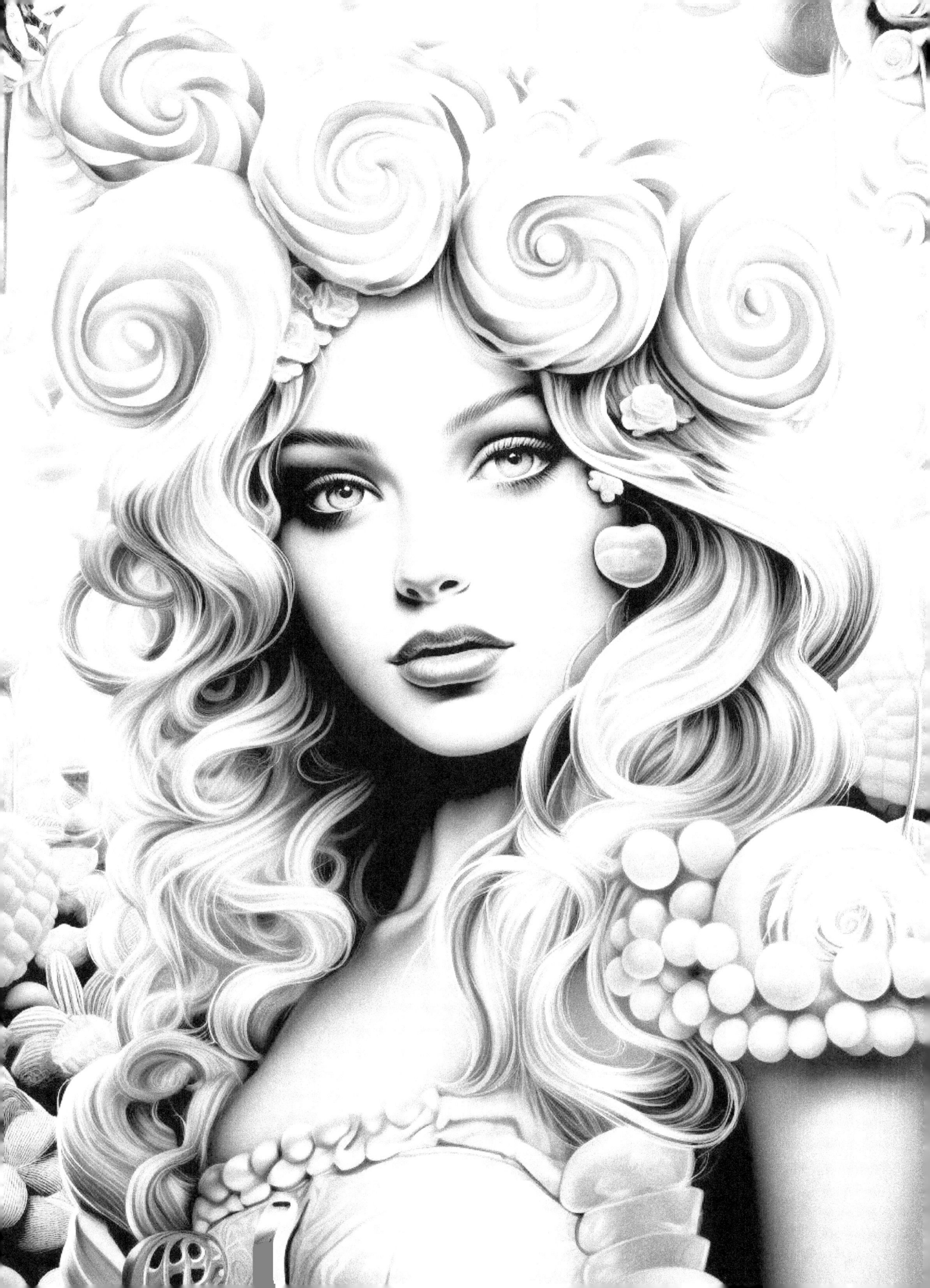

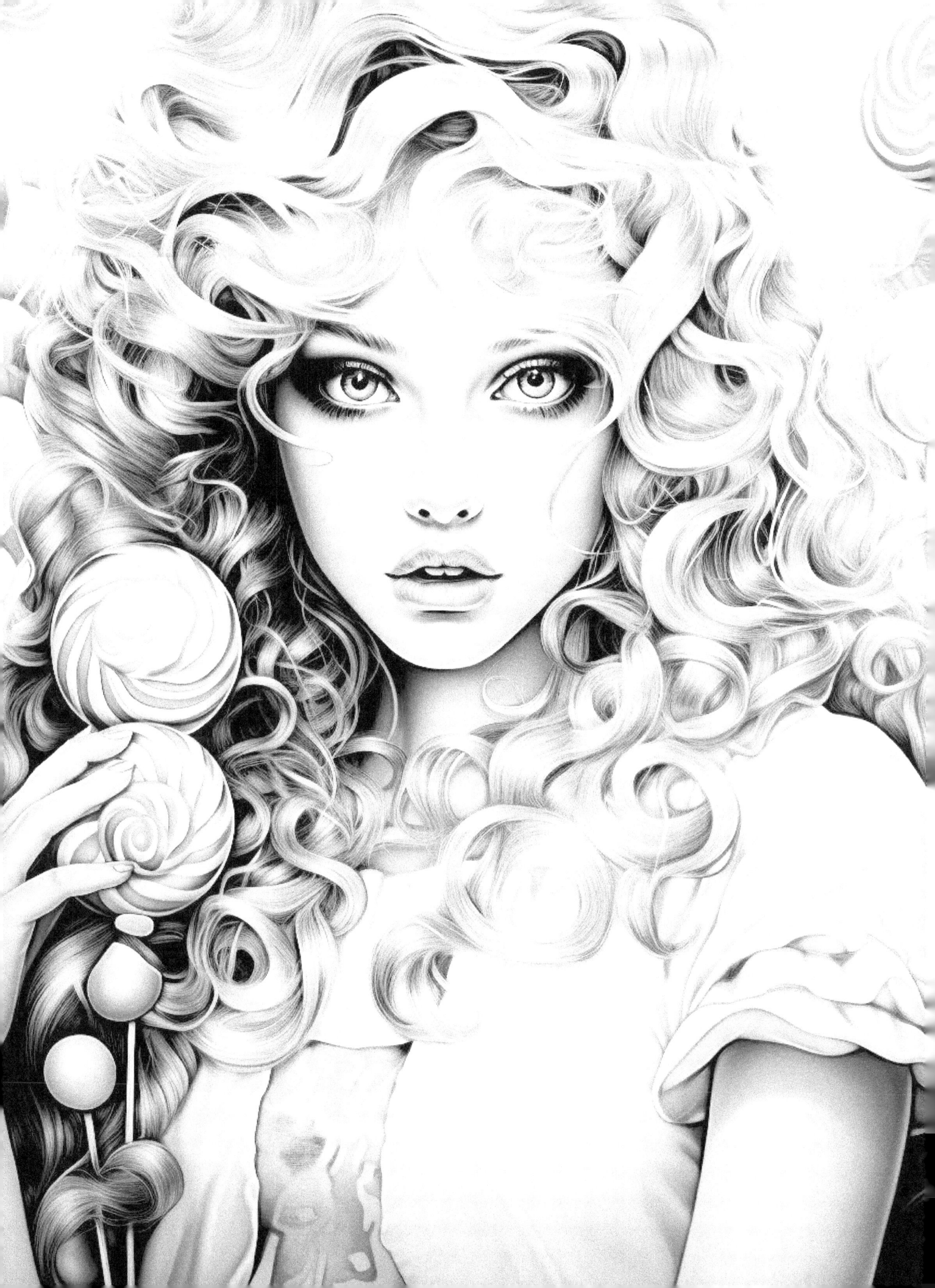

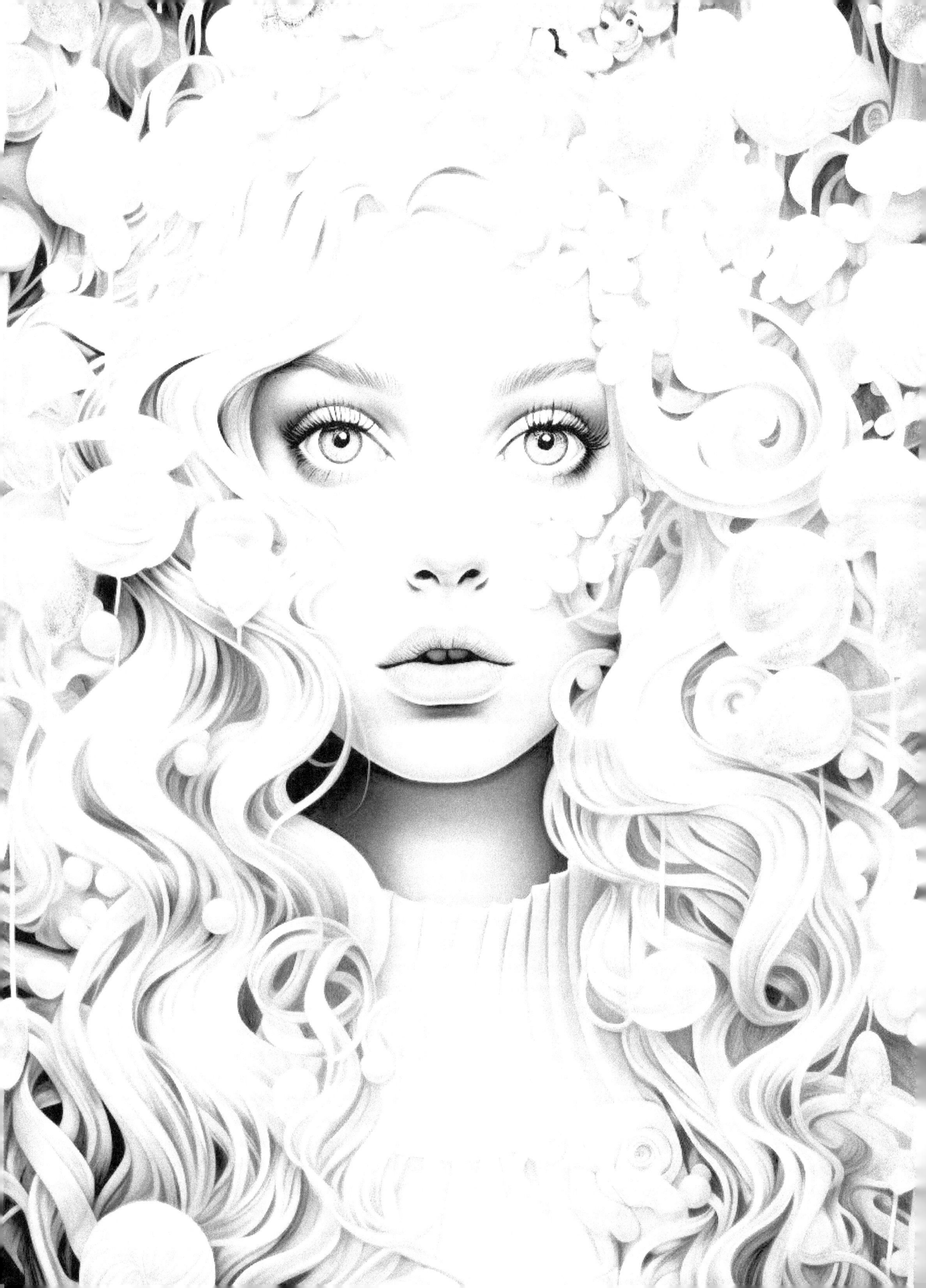

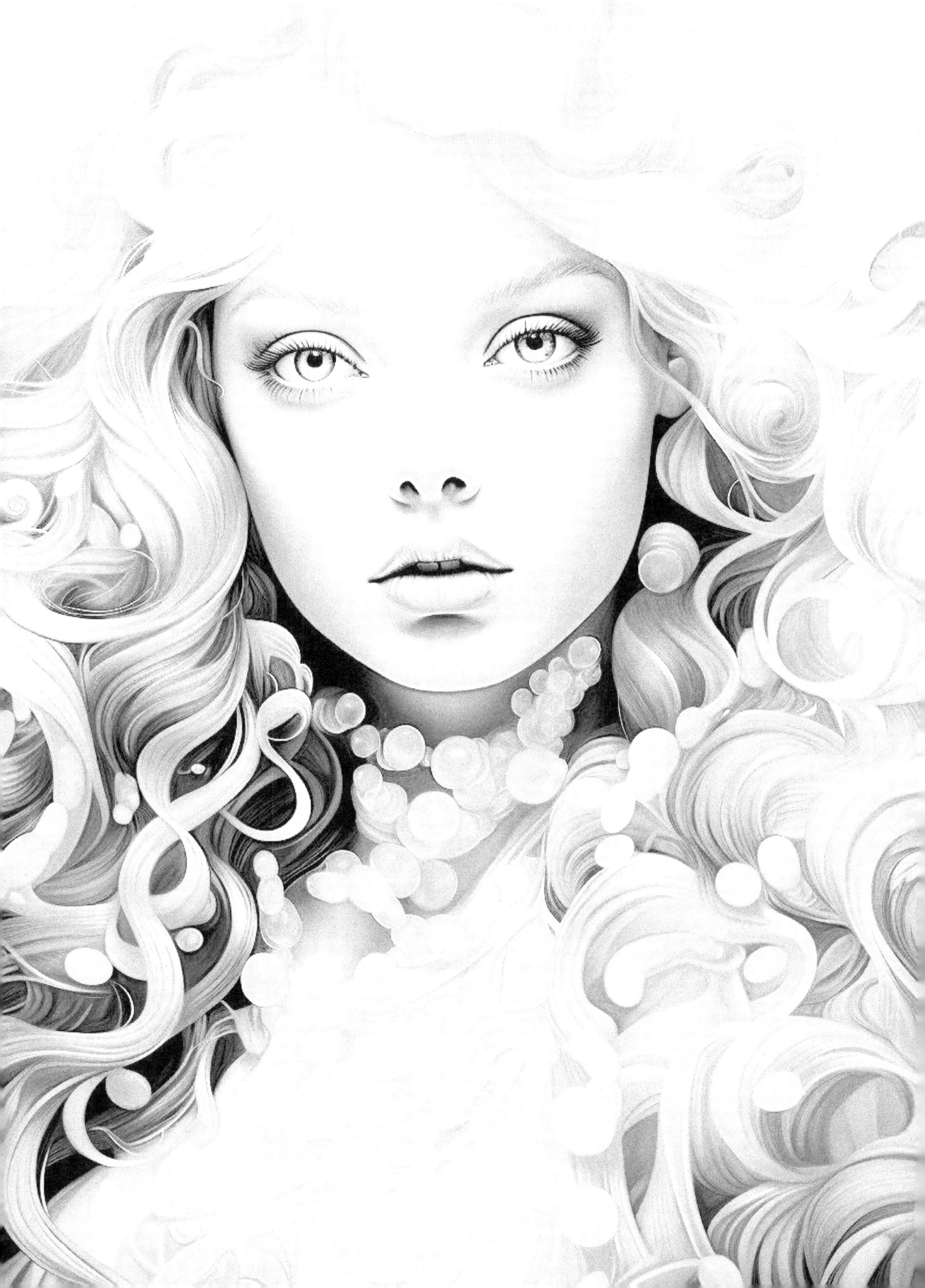

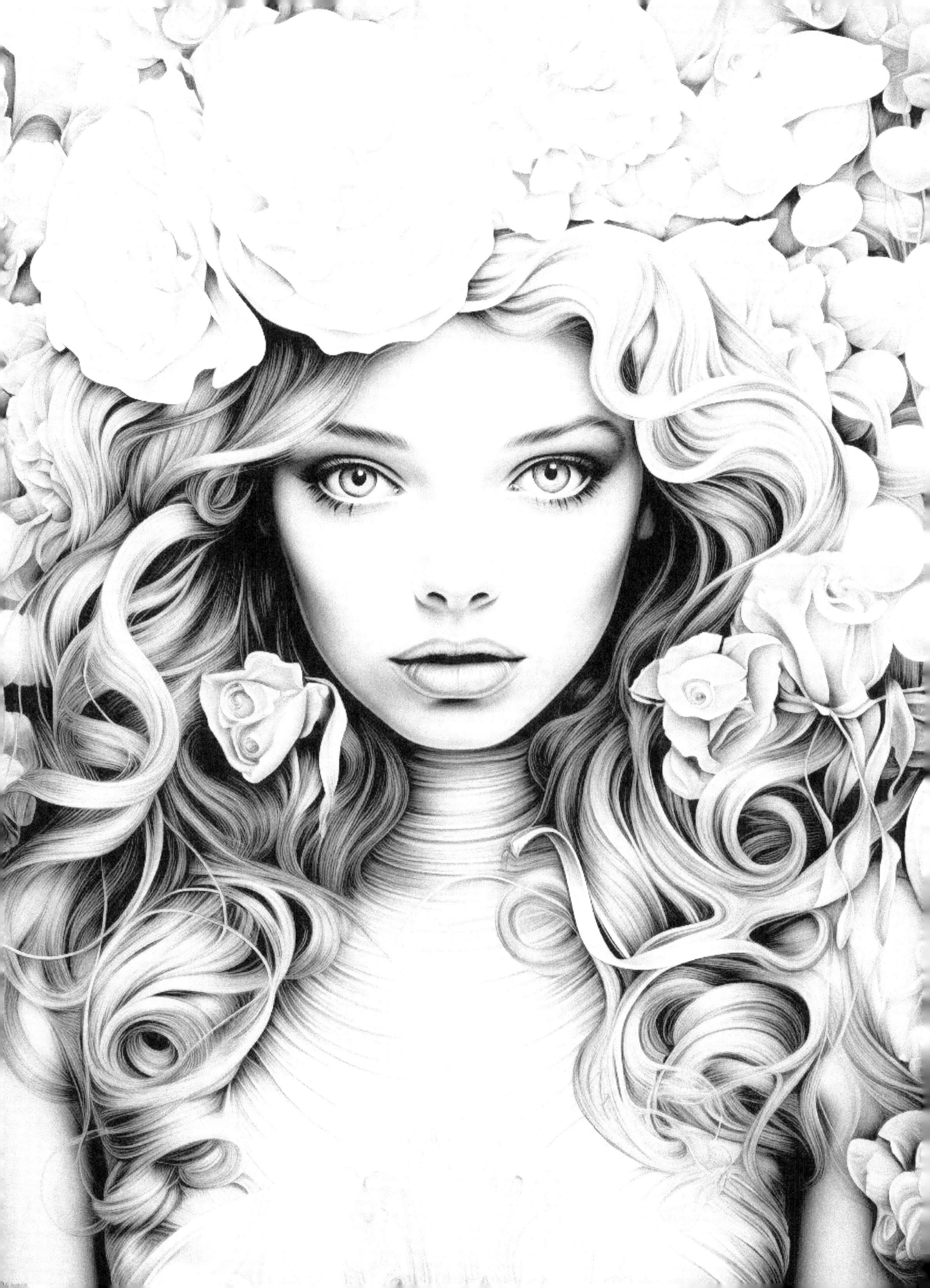

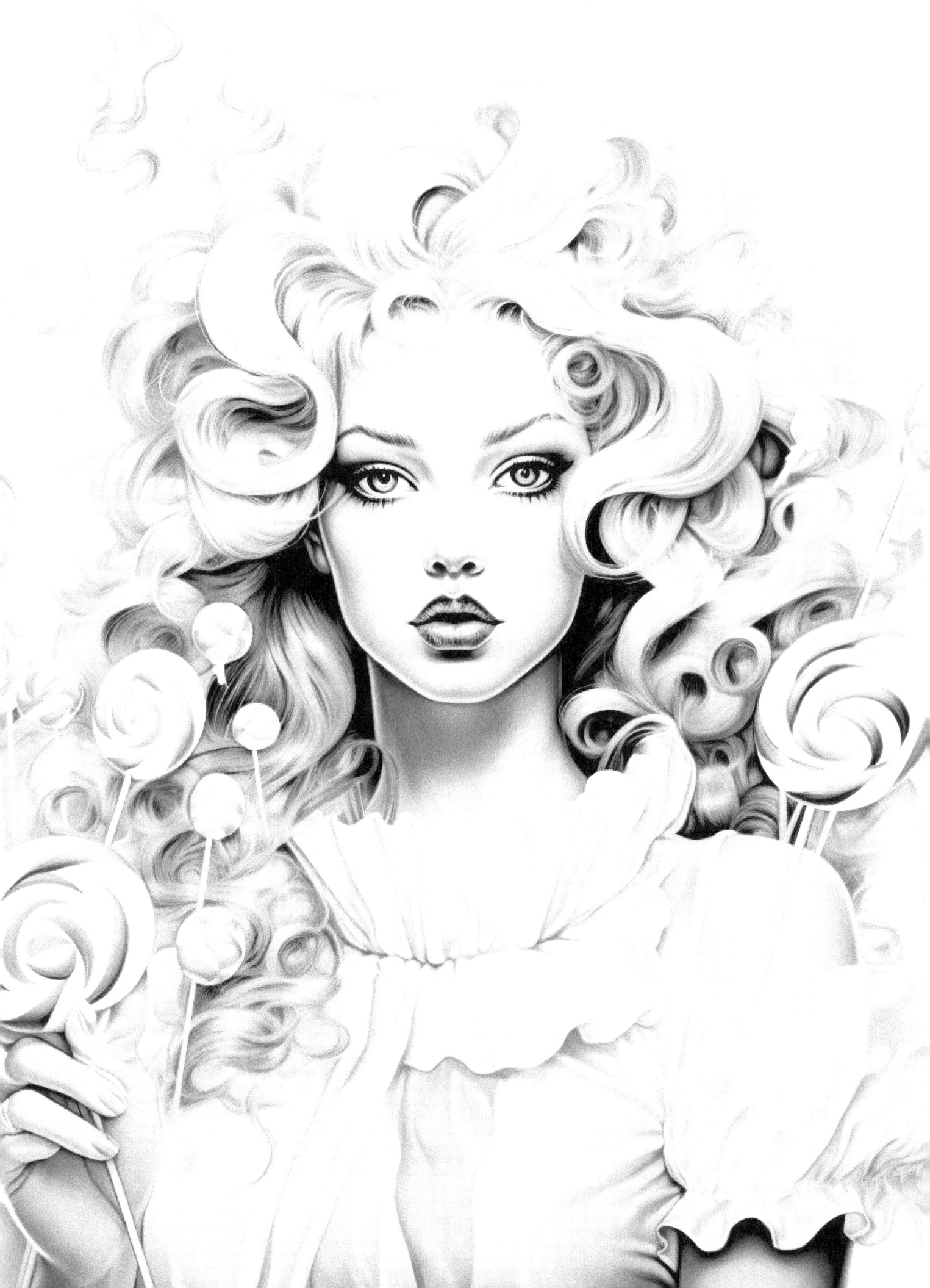

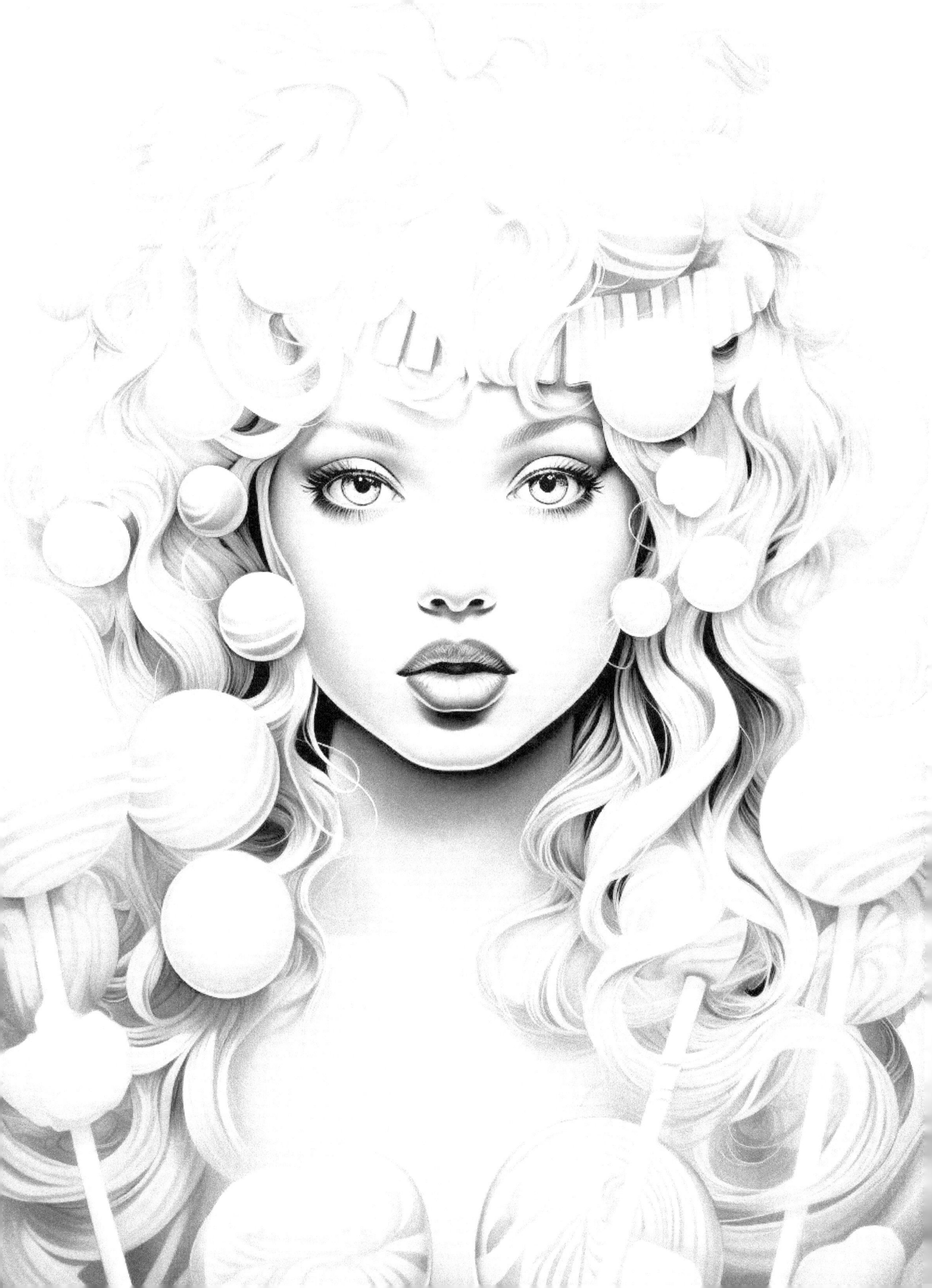

"If you enjoyed our product, it would be greatly appreciated if you could leave a review so others can receive the same benefits you have. Your review will help us see what is and what isn't working so we can serve you better and all our other customers even more."

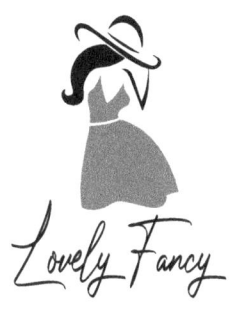

Lovely Fancy

For more beautiful books
Please scan the QR code to access
the Amazon page

Feminine Elegance Across Cultures: A Timeless Portrait Coloring Books

Fantasy Femmes: Pretty Women's Portraits Coloring Journey

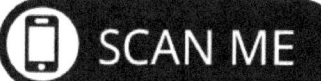